Speed Roundabouts

ENDORSEMENTS

"AN HONEST AND ENCOURAGING READ of negotiating through the contours of life."
—**Ido Drent**
Actor, New Zealand

"I HAVE JUST FINISHED READING Pip McCracken's book, *Speed Bumps and Roundabouts*. Having been in Pastoral ministry for over four decades I have gathered a library of thousands of books and have probably read thousands more on top of those. So many of them contain great, inspiring, even heroic stories. Often I have found myself admiring an author's experiences and victories and yet strangely the admiration never translated into an attempt to imitate. Their victorious stories just seemed to be beyond me somehow. "Nice to be them, sad to be me," I have thought countless times. Pip's book had an altogether different effect on me. Her honesty and vulnerability in dealing with the 'Speed Bumps and Roundabouts' in her life encouraged me to address my own. There were inspirational portions, possibly even heroic portions, but mostly the book left me feeling that this I could imitate, this is within my reach. Vulnerable, authentic people seem to have that effect on us. I think that if you read about Pip's journey through her 'Speed Bumps and Roundabouts,' you will be encouraged in facing yours."
—**Don Barry**
Senior Leader, Gateway Church, Hamilton, NZ

"WHAT STRIKES ME ABOUT PIP'S writing is the bravery woven throughout it - her willingness to be vulnerable before us, the reader, is striking & beautiful. And so I've no doubt her story will inspire bravery & hope in those who journey with her as they read."
—**JUDE HILL**
Journalist, Northern Ireland

"THERE IS SOMETHING INFECTIOUS ABOUT questions, they just draw you in and from the get-go Pip's questions make you want to keep reading. I am sure some of her questions will resonate with yours but regardless it's a story I want to read and trust that God might speak to me as I do. "
—**HELEN WARNOCK**
General Director Scripture Union Northern Ireland

Speed Bumps & Roundabouts

Lessons I've Learned on the Journey

Pip McCracken

Ambassador International
Greenville, South Carolina & Belfast, Northern Ireland
www.ambassador-international.com

Speed Bumps and Roundabouts
Lessons I've Learned on the Journey

© 2014 by Pip McCracken

All rights reserved

Printed in the United States of America

ISBN: 978-1-62020-248-7
eISBN: 978-1-62020-347-7

Unless otherwise indicated, THE HOLY BIBLE, NEW INTERNATIONAL VERSION®, NIV® Copyright © 1973, 1978, 1984, 2011 by Biblica, Inc.™ Used by permission. All rights reserved worldwide.

Scripture quotations from The Authorized (King James) Version. Rights in the Authorized Version in the United Kingdom are vested in the Crown. Reproduced by permission of the Crown's patentee, Cambridge University Press.

Scripture quotations marked (CEV) are from the Contemporary English Version Copyright © 1991, 1992, 1995 by American Bible Society, Used by Permission.

Scripture taken from the New Century Version®. Copyright © 2005 by Thomas Nelson, Inc. Used by permission. All rights reserved.

Scripture taken from The Message. Copyright © 1993, 1994, 1995, 1996, 2000, 2001, 2002. Used by permission of NavPress Publishing Group.

Scripture taken from the HOLY BIBLE, TODAY'S NEW INTERNATIONAL VERSION ® TNIV ® Copyright © 2001, 2005 by Biblica www.biblica.com. All rights reserved worldwide.

Scripture quotations marked (NLT) are taken from the Holy Bible, New Living Translation, copyright © 1996, 2004, 2007 by Tyndale House Foundation. Used by permission of Tyndale House Publishers, Inc., Carol Stream, Illinois 60188. All rights reserved.

Cover design and typesetting: Matthew Mulder
E-book conversion: Anna Riebe

AMBASSADOR INTERNATIONAL
Emerald House
427 Wade Hampton Blvd.
Greenville, SC 29609, USA
www.ambassador-international.com

AMBASSADOR BOOKS
The Mount
2 Woodstock Link
Belfast, BT6 8DD, Northern Ireland, UK
www.ambassadormedia.co.uk

The colophon is a trademark of Ambassador

*To each person mentioned on these pages
For being part of the turbulent journey;
And to you, the one who picks up these pages;
You are not the only one who has ever felt like you feel.
Keep going.*

Table of Contents

Acknowledgements — 13
Prologue — 15
   Speed Bumps and Roundabouts

CHAPTER 1
I am the sum of my story — 19
   ...on telling your story

CHAPTER 2
Stepping over the edge — 27
   ... on fear

CHAPTER 3
Under Construction — 33
   ...on being good enough

CHAPTER 4
Things I learned from movies and why they're not true — 39
   ...on how life is supposed to look

CHAPTER 5
Shalom and Sehnsucht — 45
   ...on wholeness and longing

CHAPTER 6
Every new beginning comes from some other beginning's end — 51
   ... on change

CHAPTER 7
Sometimes you know, sometimes you don't — 57
   ... on God's will

CHAPTER 8
In search of the greenest grass   63
  ... on running away

CHAPTER 9
Swings, slides and seesaws   69
  ... on choices

CHAPTER 10
Fuzzy feelings and arranged marriage   75
  ... on the meaning of love

CHAPTER 11
"Pongs" about mixed signals   81
  ... on flirting

CHAPTER 12
Kelly and Hannah   87
  ...on personality types

CHAPTER 13
From Lynne to David   91
  ... on friendship

CHAPTER 14
My cup overflows   97
  ... on jealousy and gratitude

CHAPTER 15
No feeling, no hurt   103
  ... on apathy

CHAPTER 16
Depression   109
  ... on depression

CHAPTER 17
The fingers of a 500-pound gorilla   113
  ... on pain

CHAPTER 18
Getting over it 119
... on blame

CHAPTER 19
A new definition 125
... on missions

CHAPTER 20
An Olympic silver medal 131
... on success and failure

CHAPTER 21
Movie in my mind 137
... on guarding your heart

CHAPTER 22
How not to be single 143
... on singleness

CHAPTER 23
The control of a situation 149
... on peace

CHAPTER 24
Those who pluck the fruits at the wrong time 155
... on patience

CHAPTER 25
First of July 163
... on letting go

CHAPTER 26
A god who dangles carrots? 169
... on hope

CHAPTER 27
Eagles in Zimbabwe 175
... on beauty

CHAPTER 28
If only you could see yourself as I see you   181
    ... *on humility*

CHAPTER 29
Confessions of a doormat   187
    ... *on healthy boundaries*

CHAPTER 30
Engraved   195
    ... *on being forgotten*

CHAPTER 31
Genie in a bottle   201
    ... *on answering prayers*

CHAPTER 32
524 photos   207
    ... *on remembering*

CHAPTER 33
The distance between   215
    ... *on thin places*

CHAPTER 34
Too much information?   219
    ... *on vulnerability*

CHAPTER 35
It goes on   225
    ... *on life*

Epilogue   229
    further along the road

Notes   231

Acknowledgements

Speed Bumps and Roundabouts started as a few jumbled thoughts floating around my head and has only become what you read with the help of a lot of people.

Jan – thank you for helping me to unjumble those thoughts. Most of these words would never have been made clear if it weren't for many hours with you.

Dad – thank you for your encouragement. There are many worse things I could be known as than "Alistair McCracken's daughter."

Mum – thank you for your practical help, feedback, and grammar corrections! And for inspiring me.

Sarah, Big Sister – thank you for loving books and musicals and cats and *Friends* and *Pop Idol*, from where a lot of my thoughts have come.

David – thank you for being a constant source of encouragement.

My girls, KA, Ferg, Ruthie, Julie (aka Fergannip McBriggson) – thank you for living through a lot of this stuff with me, for your honesty, for your love from the other side of the world, for always wanting to "home in."

Kelly – thank you for adventures, for sharing your family, for not laughing at me when I said I wanted to take a day off to write. (Abby, Jason, Eli, Lydia, Stan, Helen – thank you too.)

Alice – thank you for inspiring me with conversation and food, especially deep-fried mozzarella. I wish my writing was as eloquent and my food as tasty as yours!

Georgina – thank you for celebratory sushi and your excitement.

Lynne – thank you for being there since forever ago, even through the moping days.

Linley – thank you for my Wednesdays, my time to write.

My South Africans, I can't mention you all, but I need to especially thank Di and Mac – you brought colour to my life.

Shelly and Ryan – thank you for always welcoming me, for being my oldest friends in New Zealand, for believing I could do this. Thank you, Ryan, for the amazing website and for just taking it and rolling with it without my having to even ask.

Ruth and Dave – thank you for doing wonders with a camera.

Thank you to everyone who read and gave me feedback on parts of the book – Mum, Dad, Julie, Lee, Sarah, Jan, Sam.

All at Ambassador International – thank you for believing in these words and running with it. It's incredibly exciting to be able to go down this road with a company that has its roots in Northern Ireland.

Prologue

Speed Bumps and Roundabouts

I LIVE ON A ROAD that is 1.4 kilometres long.

To travel these 1400 metres right now, I have to go through three sets of road works.

For some reason, the council has decided that the best use of the taxpayers' money is to put two new roundabouts and a few speed bumps on our quiet, suburban street. This process, the building of these traffic-calming measures, is causing me to slow down as I drive from one end to the other.

I don't like to slow down.

I'm not saying that I'm a crazy, fast driver. If I said that, my friends would laugh. A lot. Me and my car (affectionately known as "the Bubble," "the nana car," or "the lunchbox"), we don't go so fast. But we have found our pace, an appropriate pace. Maybe not a fast pace, but definitely a steady pace. Roundabouts and speed bumps are disagreeable because they limit our ability to go at that pace.

I definitely don't like to be limited . . .

But I'm learning . . .

I'm learning that limitation isn't always what it seems, but that most of the time, it is what you make of it.

If life is a road, it isn't a smooth one and more often than not, we can't choose the pace at which we travel on it. Sometimes, we're puttering along, quite content. Sometimes, it seems as if we're not even moving forward. Sometimes, everyone else is whizzing past us in their four-wheel drives that don't even feel the speed bumps. And sometimes, that makes us want to pull over, say "it's not fair," and give up on the journey.

But we're never going to get to the end of the road if we stop moving, if we give up at the first obstacle. Easier said than done, I know.

Without a doubt, I know that.

As I start on the road to writing this book, writing down my thoughts and the lessons I'm learning, I don't start from a place of satisfaction, a place of having all the answers, a place of fulfilment or maybe even contentment. I start from a place of brokenness. I start with a heart that sometimes holds onto hope by only the weakest of threads. The past two, maybe three, years have been hard on my heart. In the previous five, ten, fifteen years, things happened: things that left cracks in my heart, but it seems that in the past couple of years, though no major events occurred, the cracks have been getting wider. The attrition process has deepened the wounds, insidiously eating away at the wholeness that, I think, once existed.

So, why do I write? Why write about being broken if I don't know how to fix it? Why tell people the problems if I can't tell them the answers? The answer is this: I believe that there are answers. And I hope I will find them. Maybe I'll find them as I write. Maybe not. Right now, I have more questions than answers, but I hope for answers. I hope for healing and reclaimed wholeness. I hope for the things that will help me keep on journeying down the road, keep on going through the roundabouts, over the speed bumps.

I hope for you as well. One of my greatest wishes with my writing has always been that by telling people about the things I've been through, the things I've felt, they will know that they're not alone. Through so many of these things, I have completely believed that I'm the only one ever to struggle with them. Realising that I'm not has been a breath of relief. And I hope that I can give that to you as well.

That hope is what allows me to write.

CHAPTER 1

I am the sum of my story

...on telling your story

To tell your story is to give a gift. A vulnerable gift. A gift that may be hard to give, but a gift that may give direction to the lost, breath to the drowning, relief to the hurting, life to the dying.

WE ALL HAVE A STORY.

Some are longer than others.

Some are harder to tell, harder to hear than others.

Some make you cry; some make you laugh.

And the only thing that each story has in common is that it is unique. No other person has lived your story; no other person ever will.

Actually, maybe our stories have one more thing in common . . .

. . . our stories need to be told . . .

When I was 17, I went with a group of young people to the Philippines. A couple of months before leaving, the team got together to get acquainted and talk about the trip: the purpose, practicalities, ideas, fears. As part of this training weekend, we had the opportunity to share our testimonies with each other. I was nervous about everyone looking at me as I spoke and nervous about what to say. To me, *testimony* was a grand, Christian word meaning dramatic, impressive story. I thought of great people standing before great congregations, testifying to the amazing wonders God had done in their lives. I thought of stories of missionaries who had been in the thick of poverty, on the brink of disaster, and how God had delivered them. I thought of drug addicts whose lives had been turned around and made unrecognisable from what they previously had.

But I didn't think of me.

In my mind, my story was that I grew up with Christian parents, went to church and Sunday school, became a Christian when I was six, and had some days when I didn't feel like being a Christian but mostly just did it because it was expected.

Not a very grand story.

As we shared our testimonies that weekend, I began to see that my story was dramatic, was important, was breathtaking, because it was a story about how God saved me and how He still saves me every day. I always thought that it would be much cooler if I'd been a real rebel—got drunk, broke the law, slept around—and Jesus had saved me from that. But, gradually, I saw that my story is so much better than that . . . because every day I live is part of the story of how Jesus has saved me from depression, rejection, fear, jealousy, and self-pity.

And that's only the beginning.

A few years after that trip, I was with another group, with another opportunity to tell my story. There was a group of maybe twelve of us, a newly formed committee. One by one, we told each other the tales of how we ended up there and then. I'm not sure how long it took; all I remember is that nobody cared where the time was going. As person after person shared their struggles and their triumphs and how God had been at the centre of each of them, we laughed and cried and saw how each person had been made who he or she was on that day.

Nobody else has my story.

Nobody has been through what I have.

Nobody has learned exactly the things I've needed to learn.

People love to hear stories of dramatic conversions, but they also love to hear stories of people just like them, people with real struggles, people who thought no one else in the world had their struggles. All stories have power because they were all written by the All-powerful One.

So, let me tell you a bit of my story.

My full name is Philippa Ludmilla McCracken[1], which, apparently my parents saw no problems with. Unfortunately.

I grew up in Belfast, Northern Ireland, a few years after the worst of "The Troubles."[2] I had Christian parents, who had also grown up in Northern Ireland, and I had one sister, Sarah, who was two years older than I was. I had three living grandparents, and we weren't too rich or too poor. Life was pretty standard. It was comfortable.

My parents took me to church and Sunday school, and in the holidays, Sarah and I would go to Christian camps and beach missions. At a young age (maybe four or five), I understood that God had created me, Jesus loved me (this I know, for the Bible tells me so), I was a sinner but Jesus died for me, and I needed him to live in my heart. Oh and there was something in there about trying to be good too.

I was a fairly normal, well-adjusted, seven-year-old girl until my parents divorced. I didn't even know the word *divorce* until a long time after that. All I knew was that my mum and dad were going to live in separate houses because they didn't love each other anymore, but they still loved Sarah and me. I was sad to start with, but after a bit of adjustment, I thought it was actually quite cool that I got to have two bedrooms, two birthdays, and two Christmases. Sarah and I would stay with my mum during the week and my dad on the weekends. And that's how it was for years. Little did I know that issues were being formed, ready to bite me later on in life.

In my first year of high school, I became a bit of a rebel. Thankfully, there were only so many ways that an eleven-year-old could rebel. I made the wrong friends and realised that it wasn't cool to be a

Christian. It was definitely not cool to go to the school Christian group at lunchtime. It was cool to swear, to make fun of people, to make sure they knew that we were much cooler than they were. I was still a well-behaved Christian when I was at home, but not so much when I was with Kimberly, Tara, and Kelly.

Halfway through that year, I went on a weekend away with the school Christian group, probably to keep my dad happy. During that weekend, I had my first experience of understanding the reality of what Jesus did for me and what it meant for my life. It was the first time that I cried because of it. I remember it clearly; it happened during one of the songs that the band was singing. It just hit me, and I knew I had to sort myself out. I spoke to one of the leaders through my sobs and left that weekend resolutely deciding that things were going to change.

I didn't lead a perfect life after that, but I did live knowing what path I wanted to go down. I made some new friends at school, friends I believe God put in the right place at the right time. As we grew up through school, I learned about being independent in my faith, I learned that sometimes the easiest thing is not the right thing, and I learned that people change.

Just before my penultimate year of school, I left to complete my education at a different school. There, I met Tim (not his real name), and we had a relationship that lasted a few months. He was my first boyfriend. We broke up on good terms, agreeing that, while we were good friends, we weren't a great couple. I believed him when he told me that—even though it wasn't exactly what I was feeling. A few weeks later, he officially started dating my best friend, Laura (not her real name). It knocked me. Ha, the people I was close to at that stage would know what an understatement that was. I felt rejected, not good enough. It hurt, and I had no idea how to handle it. My friendships with both of them were in tatters, and my final year of school was endured more than enjoyed. I was angry with God. When I found out about Tim and Laura, my first thought was "Why would God do this to me?" Throughout the next few months, those thoughts turned into "Why isn't God taking away these feelings of hurt? Why won't God just make them break up? Why do I have to see them together all the time? Why did God make me go out with him in the first place? Does God even care about me?" Those thoughts stayed at the back of my mind, but I repressed them and carried on.

After leaving school, I took a gap year, spending the first few months working a monotonous office job before going to South Africa to work with Scripture Union.[3] The six-and-a-bit months I spent there were one of the most significant times in my life to date. I grew more in those few months than I had in my previous 18 years. There is much to tell about that, but not just yet . . .

I returned from South Africa a different person and found it incredibly difficult to get back into life at home. I spent a long time just wanting to be back in South Africa. Every Sunday night I would spend a couple of hours on the phone to my South African friends. Northern Ireland had changed while I'd been away, the most major thing being that my mum had moved to England to be with Tony, the man she would marry a few years later.

I started university about a month after I came home. I studied a four-year honours degree in physiotherapy. I had some amazing times and some hideous times. At uni, I met Kerryann, Catherine, Ruth, and Julie (all their real names), the four girls who, I'm pretty sure, will be my friends no matter how much time goes past and no matter how much distance there is between us. We lived together for the last three years of uni and had some hilarious times, ate some great food (Cat's brownies were always a winner, even the time she accidentally used chilli oil in them), went on some exciting holidays, and laughed and cried a lot. Happy, happy times.

Uni was difficult. I didn't enjoy my degree. I had done well at school, but at uni, I felt like a small fish in a big pond. I was not a naturally gifted physio and had to work incredibly hard to keep my head above water and achieve the standard I thought I should. During the last couple of years, my goal was to finish my degree as well as I could and after that, I would work out what to do. I was almost sure it wouldn't be physiotherapy. Aside from not enjoying it, jobs were extremely scarce in Northern Ireland.

By chance, I saw an advert in a physio magazine for physio jobs in New Zealand. Sometimes, I'm not entirely sure what possessed me to move to the other side of the world to do a job I didn't really want to do, but that's exactly what I did. Four years later, I'm still in New Zealand, in Hamilton.

In the last four years in New Zealand, I have changed jobs after being made redundant from my first, I have lived in six different flats, I have worked with several different rugby teams, and I have travelled around a lot of NZ, as well as to Niue and Australia.

And I have started to heal.

It took me until I was 26 to realise that I had issues that weren't going to go away unless I actively sought to make them. So I started seeing a counsellor, and I started making changes, all with God's help. And the healing started. I still have a long way to go, but I'm on the right track.

So where I'm at right now is in a changing state of being settled. This year, I have decided to work four days a week, taking Wednesdays off to work on things that I love—writing, being creative, making cards, resting. It's allowing me to have more time and energy to spend with people that I want to devote time to, after being overwhelmingly busy in the last few years. It's refocusing me, giving me new joy and passion to carry on down the road.

When I look back, I see that I've had some pretty dumb stuff happen in my life. I've had it good much of the time, but sometimes not.

And when I look back, I do see that God is good; He has always been good. All the time. That gives me confidence that He always will be.

So, there you have it.

That's my story . . . for now anyway.

CHAPTER 2

Stepping over the edge

...on fear

If there is no fear, I seriously doubt that there is understanding. If there is no fear, there cannot be growth. If there is no fear, what is there to conquer?

THERE I WAS, 18 YEARS old, sitting in Belfast City Airport[1], trying not to let all the strangers around me see the tears streaming down my face. Hood pulled over my head, looking at the floor, I wondered what on earth had possessed me to get to this point. Whose stupid idea was it to leave the security of home to go to a country that everybody knew was dangerous? Oh, that's right; it was mine. At that moment, why I'd ever thought it was a good idea escaped me.

I was terrified. Standing on the edge of six months in South Africa, I was just plain terrified. It seemed that everyone I met was determined to scare me out of going. Whenever I told someone I was going to South Africa, they seemed to take great pleasure in telling me about their third cousin twice removed or their best friend's uncle's son who got mugged fourteen times within half an hour as he walked through Durban. Or they would tell me matter-of-factly that Johannesburg was one of the most dangerous cities in the world. And if I survived being mugged, well, I'd probably get rabies or typhoid or maybe be bitten by a deadly poisonous snake. And if the doctors managed to heal me, on the way home from the hospital, I'd probably be in a car crash with one of the innumerable drunk drivers.

I was terrified.

By the time I arrived at the airport, all my instincts told me to turn around and go home where I would be safe, where everything was familiar. The fearmongers' words were cycling through my mind, and I was convinced that anything that could go wrong would go wrong. Between being sure I would get lost in Heathrow or be unable to find my travel companions[2] or lose all my belongings or the plane would be hijacked, I was amazed to find myself on the plane, listening to the safety announcement, heading to Johannesburg.

There are many things I could tell you about the six months I spent volunteering for Scripture Union in Port Shepstone, on the South Coast of Kwa-Zulu Natal in South Africa. Things I could tell you about the lessons I learned, the ways I grew, the ways I changed, the impact that six months had on my life: there is no way I could fit those things into one chapter. It would be a miniscule overview of the seven journals I filled while I was there! But I have to introduce you to this period of my life, because it was one of the most significant. The people I met, the things I saw, the things I did (even when I was almost too scared to do them)—I'm not sure where I would be or who I would be now if I hadn't experienced them.

Throughout most of my life, fear has dominated far too much of my decision-making. I have avoided important events because of fear. I have put off simple tasks, things as simple as a phone call to book a tennis court, because of fear. I have gotten myself worked up, stressed, even sick because of fear. But at the same time, I seem to have a button in my head that, when it's pressed, when my guard is down for five seconds, makes me jump off the cliff, head first into the fear. I must have forgotten to be scared just long enough to send the application form for South Africa, and then I was trapped. I'd stepped over the edge of the cliff, and no matter how much I screamed and yelled, there was no going back.

I was scared of everything. Sure, there were the obvious ones—snakes, spiders, guns—but I managed to have a few obscure fears as well: fainting and phone calls, to name a couple. I was scared of people, especially foreign people. Not scared that they were going to murder me as I slept or anything like that, more that they wouldn't like me, they would think I was an idiot, or I would embarrass myself in front of them or offend them or hurt them. I was scared of being the centre of attention, even in a small group. When there were too many people looking at me, or too much attention on me, I would go a very interesting shade of red.

I think South Africa wanted to cure me of this fear using flood therapy: from the second I arrived, I was surrounded by people I didn't know, people who struggled to understand my accent, close knit families that I wanted to please, people with cultural differences that I didn't understand.

I had spent a lot of my teenage years avoiding attention, avoiding speaking in front of people. I didn't have the luxury of this avoidance in South Africa. During my time there, I had to lead devotions, school Christian groups, discussion groups, and camps, and I had to stand up at the front of church.

Shortly after I arrived, I was told that I would be responsible for the organising and running of a kids' camp toward the end of my time there. I made every effort to push that knowledge to the back of my head in order to stop myself dreading it every second of every day till it happened. I would have to phone people, go to schools to advertise, find leaders, lead the leaders, and speak in front of the group of kids. It was just not something I did!

Another thing that was not on my to-do list was visiting a country whose violence and corruption regularly landed it a spot on the news. I liked to stay out of dangerous places. All I knew of Zimbabwe was from the media: violence, death, and other things that I didn't want to be anywhere near. But someone had told me before I left for South Africa that I should accept every invitation I got, so when Shelly, who I was working and staying with, invited me to go for a holiday to her home town of Harare, I quickly said yes; quickly so I couldn't think about it too much.

Then were the standard fears: the fear that a black mamba would slither into my room and bite me as I slept, the fear that we would get hijacked driving home through the gorge at night, the fear of being hit by a taxi, and on and on. At times, the fears were almost crippling, if not stopping me from doing things, at least making me seem ridiculous and annoying to a lot of my friends.

Thankfully, God began to work.

There were a lot of deep breaths, a lot of prayers, a lot of panicked moments, but I did it, and I kept doing it. I kept stepping out, facing the fear and growing each time I realised that my fear was nothing in God's presence. I say that easily when I look back, but most of the time, it was far from easy, and the fear did not feel like nothing. In every situation, it felt very real, but I learned that, although God doesn't often take away the fear, He is there as you step into it, even if He is only visible when you look back over your shoulder.

So I did the things that scared me: I led discussion groups, discovering that I loved listening to teenagers open up; I stood up in front of the church, discovering that being involved in a powerful service changed my life too; I organised and led a camp, learning that I had skills that God could use; and I went to Zimbabwe, to discover an incredible country, a beautiful country with elephants and fresh fish and creamy orange sunsets and people filled with hope in spite of the pain of the past.

When I left South Africa, a little over six months after I arrived, I was different. I had come to the country walking with baby steps, tentatively feeling the ground in front of me, looking around me to do whatever I could to make sure I was safe, free of embarrassment, and free of failure. I left the country looking ahead, striding ahead, confident, or at least on my way to confidence. Erica, the mother of the family I stayed with, had some words for me before I left. She told me that she remembered the first night that I walked into her house, looking scared and pale and as if I was about to cry (I had melted down a bit that first night, which I had hoped had gone unnoticed—apparently not), but Erica told me that she now saw a brave and confident girl standing in front of her. Maybe I didn't even recognise it till Erica said it. The growing confidence, the fear fading—it was something I hadn't seen happening, but when I looked back, I could see how and where it happened. Every time I had stepped into something that scared me silly, every time I realised that God was already there for my next step, those were the times I grew.

After being in South Africa for about a month, somehow (I'm still not quite sure how), someone convinced me to do the Oribi Gorge Rope Swing[3], the world's highest gorge swing. The farm we stayed on wasn't far from the swing, so I knew all about its existence. And I was determined to stay away from it. So, I'm still not quite sure how I found myself standing on the edge of the gorge, the heavy rope attached to my waist, but there I was. Twelve inches in front of me, the ground disappeared. Cold sweat from a combination of nerves and the scorching heat poured off me as I held on tightly to the thick rope that was soon to be my only point of contact with solid ground.

"Ready?"

I don't remember my answer to what seemed like a silly question. How could I ever be ready to throw myself off a cliff to freefall ninety metres toward the bottom of this beautiful but deep gorge? An array of thoughts circulated in my head, blocking out the rest of the world: how had they managed to convince me to do the world's highest rope swing? What would it feel like to hurtle toward the ground? How loudly would I scream? Would my shoes fall off?!

I drifted back to reality, realising that it didn't really matter how ready I felt . . .

"Three . . . two . . . one . . .!"

"Ahhhhhhhhhhhhhhhhhhhhhhhhhhhhhhhhhhhhh!!!!!!!!!"

If I had waited till I thought I was ready or till the fear went away, I never would have taken that step, I never would have experienced the thrill of the freefall, and I never would have known the relief of realising that the rope was strong enough to hold me.

CHAPTER 3

Under construction

. . . on being good enough

Being enough is a human concept that breeds guilt and low self-esteem. Under its control, we strive for what we cannot achieve, because how can we become something we already are?

ENOUGH IS A FUNNY WORD. How much is enough? Is it subjective, or can it be measured? Is enough the same for you as for me? Who determines enough—the person giving or the person receiving?

Enough has been a constant struggle throughout my life. I've had goals, mostly self-imposed but heavily influenced by the people around me. At different points of life, I have felt not smart enough, not pretty enough, not talented enough, not creative enough, not brave enough, not exciting enough, not friendly enough, not cool enough . . . just not enough. *Enough* is a word that has a power over me, maybe a power that I have given it, but a power that I have battled to escape from.

Thankfully, amazingly, some years ago, I found two more words that have flashed up in my life, counteracting the power of *enough*. If there was one theme that had recurred throughout my life, one message that was the only thing I could tell people, one lesson that I thought God had been teaching me, it would be this chapter. In so many situations, in so many ways, the words *Under Construction* have shaped my life.

In my fight to be enough, I've believed that I have to be perfect . . . to be kind and generous all the time. To never be jealous or angry or impatient or selfish. To love people with a perfect, unfailing love. To never hurt anyone.

My mistake, my conflict, has come from believing that it's not okay when I mess up.

A year after my first trip to South Africa, I decided to go back to spend a month catching up with friends and taking part in some of the camps and holiday clubs I had been part of the first time around.

I had the privilege of being the group leader for a great group of grade seven girls at Merlewood Holiday Club, one of the biggest holiday programs that SU organised on the South Coast. The theme for the week was "Ground Breakers"[1]: it was all based around building and construction. All the leaders got to dress up in overalls and hard hats and mark all the group meeting areas out with demarcation tape. We even brought in a big digger one day! Part of our costume involved t-shirts that had been made locally. They were red and featured a yellow man-at-work sign with the words *Under Constructon*[2] underneath. Read the words again. See it? Look a bit closer. It wasn't till the second day that one of the helpers who had come in to take some photos asked us, "Where's the *i*? Isn't it meant to say *Under Construction*?" Oh well, maybe it highlighted the point. Nobody's perfect.

The week of holiday club was intense. There was singing, praying, talking, playing and at the end, our team was exhausted. But for a few of us involved with SU, there was no time to rest. We were straight onto the next thing on the holiday schedule: Wild in Winter teen camp. By the time it started, I was worn out and felt like I had wasted all my enthusiasm and energy in my first two weeks of ministry. I didn't want to do it. Plain and simple as that. I tried to think of many ways to get out of it, but I couldn't. I was grumpy, tired, and fed up. These feelings soon gave way to guilt. Shouldn't I be excited about doing God's work? Surely I was a horrible, ungrateful, selfish person.

The first day of camp was a disaster for me. I felt like I was a complete failure as a group leader, definitely not good enough. I was leading a group of teenage girls, and I had met most of them before. Zama, Happy, and S'tha had been at the previous year's camp; Phindile, Candice, and Ntsiki were at Merlewood Holiday Club the previous week. But it seemed that they didn't want to talk to me. They all spoke Zulu all the time. I had no objection to them speaking their own language—of course, it was only natural, but they all spoke English very well, and I wanted to be able to build relationships with them, which was difficult when the only Zulu words I knew were *sawubona* (hello) and *bhubesi* (lion).

In my head, I was listing my shortcomings and failures, all the reasons why I was a bad leader, a bad person, and why everyone else was better.

While I was in the middle of that camp, under the cloud of those thoughts, I stumbled across 2 Corinthians 12:9, which has become a source of endless encouragement since:

> My grace is sufficient for you, for my power is made perfect in weakness.

In the preceding verses, Paul tells us why God said those words to him:

> Therefore, in order to keep me from becoming conceited, I was given a thorn in my flesh, a messenger of Satan, to torment me. Three times I pleaded with the Lord to take it away from me. But he said to me, "My grace is sufficient for you, for my power is made perfect in weakness."[3]

Paul had a "thorn in his flesh." Who knows what it was? He leaves us guessing. But I knew, at that time, I had some big thorns jabbing right on into me: exhaustion, grumpiness, bitterness about God's will, inability to communicate, jealousy of other people, lack of love, and no skills (I wasn't a great speaker, I couldn't play the guitar, and I could never think of games to play). And it went on. I was just little old me.

But what I saw was that it was okay.

Because for every inch of little old me, every grain of my humanity, there was a big, great God with mounds of power and grace.

I had forgotten that it's not about me and my skills and abilities. It never has been, never will be. I wanted to make a difference on that camp, to be useful to the people around me and to God, but I forgot that I could only do that by God's grace and God's power that would work in spite of my flaws. I had to accept that I had flaws. I have to accept that every day. I began to realise that God could and would work through them at that point, but even more than that, He would continue to work on them.

Every day, through every situation, I learn and I grow. Sometimes it feels like I'm taking steps back, and sometimes I'm all too aware that I am far from perfect, but what I've come to realise is that I will never be perfect while I'm here on earth. But God has begun to work in me, and I'm confident that He will "continue His work until it is finally finished on the day Christ Jesus comes back again."[4]

God doesn't wait until we're finished, until we're perfect, to use us. If He did, He would be waiting a very long time. He uses us as we are: flawed and broken and hurting and lost. You just need a quick skim through the Bible to see the truth in that: David committed adultery, Abraham lied, Ruth was a foreigner, Peter denied he knew Jesus, Paul killed Christians, Thomas doubted, Jeremiah was young, Moses had a stutter and a lot of excuses, and Matthew cheated. But God used them all. He had to do a little work on some of them first, smooth off a few rough edges, but none of those things were big enough to stop God.

It was such a relief to me when I realised that there was nothing that I had done, nothing that I could do, nothing about my personality that could stop God.

"Every saint has a past and every sinner has a future," said Oscar Wilde[5], so stop letting guilt hold you back. Stop letting fear of failure prevent you from taking the first step. Stop letting what other people think control who you are or what you do.

God wants you.

So, don't just think that some time in the future when you're older or wiser or can control your temper or you live somewhere else or you're not single or you're a better person, you'll serve God and do what He wants. He wants all of you now, how you are. That doesn't mean He's not going to work on you or change you, but you are a work in progress. You are under construction, and you will always be. So, the time to start living for God, being used by Him?

That time is now.

CHAPTER 4

Things I learned from movies and why they're not true

...on how life is supposed to look

Maybe we don't know best. Maybe the best plans are not the ones we plan for ourselves. Maybe when things go wrong, it's because they have to take that turn to lead to another turn where things will go right. Maybe happily ever afters aren't all they're cracked up to be.

"WHAT SCREWS US UP MOST in life is the picture in our head of how it's supposed to be."[1]

When I was growing up, I knew what my life was going to look like... I would live with a happy family, go to school, have good friends, go to university to study something I loved, probably fall in love while I was at uni, find a secure job that I enjoyed every day, get married by the time I was 25, pop out a few kids, watch them grow up and have secure, happy lives, and we would all live happily ever after.

It was a good plan... if only life had followed the script.

I didn't plan for my parents to get divorced, to have to move to another school because of bullying, to dislike uni so much that

I contemplated dropping out, to move to the other side of the world, to still be single, to be made redundant.

But who puts those "perfect" ideas in our heads? Where do we get those ideas about what life is supposed to look like, what is supposed to happen? Honestly, I think a lot of it comes from movies. TV and music too, but I think movies are a big part of the problem. And growing up, the movies kids watch are the Disney ones; the stories they know are the fairytales they're based on.

Why else do little girls want to be princesses? Cinderella, Snow White, The Little Mermaid, Sleeping Beauty, Pocahontas, Beauty and the Beast; what little girl hasn't wished she was Ariel, Aurora, or Belle? The beautiful girl who has meager beginnings, who sits around, singing to the birds in the forest, waiting for Prince Charming to gallop in on his horse and finish her song. But what is that actually teaching our little girls? And our little boys?

Look at Cinderella[2]: abused by her family, an abuse that she simply accepts. She is meek and accepting, doing her work, waiting, ignoring her dreams . . . singing to animals. Until one day there is a ball, which she desperately wants to go to. And what do you know, the fairy godmother appears, the universe cuts her a break, maybe just because she wanted it so badly. She goes to the ball, the prince takes one look at her, and they fall in love. After a minor mishap with a glass slipper (which just doesn't sound comfortable, really) and a carriage returning to its pumpkiny state, the prince finds her; they get married and live happily ever after.

If I wanted to be like Cinderella, it seems that would mean accepting cruelty without question, waiting for good things to happen without actually doing anything about it. In reality, the universe does not hand us gifts just because we wait long enough for them and just because we're beautiful. Love does not happen with one glimpse. A prince does not search the kingdom for us after one brief meeting, whether we are beautiful or not. Maybe we need to decide between two philosophies: Good things come to those who wait? Or, if it's going to be, it's up to me?

Let's put Snow White[3] and Sleeping Beauty[4] together, because there's one thing their stories have in common that I think distorted the way I have dealt with a lot of relationships. Both of them are woken from near death by a kiss.

Well, not any old kiss . . . true love's first kiss, blah blah blah.

It's not just Disney who is guilty of this one. Virtually any romantic movie you can watch gives messages about kissing: a kiss is the start of a relationship, a kiss can fix a multitude of problems, a kiss equals love. It's taken me a long time to realise that those things are not always true. Sometimes kisses cause more problems than good—maybe because of the conceptions we have about them. I think boys and girls see them very differently too. To a girl, especially a romantic girl who wishes she were a Disney princess, every kiss means true love. To a boy, often a kiss is merely a rush of hormones. I know that's a bit of a generalisation, and I don't want to condemn all boys as superficial and all girls as hopeless romantics, but it might be helpful to be aware of it.

In my very first relationship, there was a lot of kissing. It made me feel attractive, wanted, loved, special. It wasn't till many years later that I realised that actually what happened was that we didn't always have much to talk about, so instead of awkward silences, we would just kiss. Not very romantic, really. I'm not saying that kissing is bad. I am definitely not saying that. I have friends who didn't kiss till they were married and other friends who kissed before they were officially a couple, and neither have turned out badly. I guess I'm saying that we just need to be honest with ourselves about what a kiss is and what it isn't. Kisses are beautiful, but they don't always mean true love.

Who's next? Oh yes, let's go under the sea. Ariel, the Little Mermaid.[5] Ariel had it all. She was the daughter of the sea king;

she was beautiful; she had whozits and whatsits galore and twenty thingamabobs. What more could a girl want? The prince, of course. So what does she do to get him, this prince that she has seen once? Oh, nothing major, just drastically changes her appearance (legs instead of a tail), gives up her family, her home, and her gifts (her voice). And somehow, it ends up okay. Yes, of course there are troubles along the way. The prince nearly marries the sea witch in disguise, Ariel nearly dies, but at the end of the day, she gets what she wants: her prince and her new life on the greener grass of the other side.

Is that okay?

Is it okay for us to believe that we will get the life we want, or the life we think we want, if we just give up everything that we are?

Surely the answer is no.

And it's not all about the girls. Let's have a look at the Hunchback of Notre Dame.[6] Finally, it looked like Disney wasn't going to be all about the beauty. The whole way through the movie, we love Quasimodo; we see his beautiful heart, his kindness and love, even though he's deformed. Then, what do you know, he doesn't get the girl. No, no, valiant, attractive Phoebus gets Esmeralda, and the hunchback is alone, cementing for us the notion that you have to be physically attractive to get the life you want.

No wonder we have such screwed-up views of how our lives are supposed to be. No wonder so many girls sit around waiting for a prince, someone who will pursue them wholeheartedly, love them unwaveringly, fight for them valiantly and look good as well. For years, whether I've admitted it or not, I've believed that life will only properly begin when I'm married. I'm beginning to see that life has already begun, life in all its fullness. Life with its ups and downs, failures and successes, joys and sorrows.

So, my life is not a Disney movie . . . you know what? Having gone through the things that have caused hurt and sadness, I'm not sure how much I would have changed about them. Because I would not be where I am or who I am now without those things. If I had stayed at the school where I was bullied, I wouldn't have made such a good friendship with Lynne or become more confident. If I had stayed with my first boyfriend, I would have been married at 21 and wouldn't have gone to South Africa. If I had studied something else, even if I loved it, I probably wouldn't have ended up in New Zealand. If I hadn't been made redundant, I never would have learned what a good employer was like.

If the bad stuff hadn't happened, I don't know whether I would have experienced as much of God's love, grace, and power. I would have known in my head that He heals broken hearts, but my heart would not have felt the reality of that.

Maybe we don't know best. Maybe the best plans are not the ones we plan for ourselves. Maybe when things go wrong, it's because they have to take that turn to lead to another turn where things will go right. Maybe happily ever afters aren't all they're cracked up to be.

Or maybe happy endings are just a concept made up by Hollywood, so it's ironic that I'm going to give you a quote from a movie about happy endings. *He's Just Not That into You* is a chick flick that is painfully honest about the lies we tell ourselves because we want to believe them and the ways our friends pander to this because they know it will make us happy in the short term. The quote I want to share is this,

> And maybe a happy ending . . . is you, on your own, picking up the pieces and starting over, freeing yourself up for something better in the future . . . just moving on. Or maybe the happy ending is this, knowing after all the unreturned phone calls, broken hearts, through the blunders and misread signals, through all the pain and embarrassment, you never gave up hope.[7]

CHAPTER 5

Shalom and Sehnsucht

... on wholeness and longing

Longing for wholeness is a far deeper affliction than I give it credit for. It is in every day. It is in every thing. It is in every person. The whisper that things are not quite as they're meant to be.

SHALOM AND SEHNSUCHT: TWO WORDS in two different languages, both notoriously difficult to translate adequately. At their most basic, *shalom* is peace and *sehnsucht* is longing, but those definitions barely scratch the surface.

I'm no language scholar, but understanding the concepts behind these two words has helped me appreciate a lot about how I feel and why I feel it.

שלום *(Shalom)*

When I was at primary school, we had assembly every week. They would pile us all into the hall and make us sit cross-legged with arms folded and eyes facing the front. Apart from that, I don't remember many details about assemblies, except the singing. I remember the piano that sat on the right-hand side of the stage that Mrs. McDowell would play as we sang our hearts out as if our educations depended on it. I remember the songs we sang—some of them, anyway. One of them introduced me to the word *shalom*. We would sing it as a round, with half the kids starting and the other half coming in halfway through. It had a jaunty Hebrew feel to it and went a little something like this:

> *Shalom, shalom*
> *May peace be with you*
> *Throughout your days*
> *In all that you do, may peace be with you*
> *Shalom, shalom*

So, for years, I knew the word *shalom,* and I knew it meant "peace." It was a long time before I discovered that peace is only the beginning when it comes to shalom. It is a word used as a greeting in Hebrew, at the start or the end of a conversation, sometimes as part of the phrase "Shalom Aleichem"—peace be upon you. However, the person who greets you with this phrase is wishing you much more than peace, much more than the absence of trouble or presence of tranquillity.

Shalom means completeness, soundness, welfare, as well as peace.[1] Completeness. That word makes me sigh a little bit; I want it so badly. And really, who wouldn't? To be living completely in the will of God with complete purpose. Completely whole, completely free, completely satisfied, completely loving, completely loved, completely happy, completely fulfilled, completely complete!

Usually, shalom seems a long way off, but there have been times when I've felt closer to it than other times, times when I haven't wanted to move from the moment I'm in. Times with friends, times in creation, times of purpose.

One of those times was when I discovered that I loved writing. After I came back from South Africa with seven journals worth of thoughts and stories, I knew I didn't want to lose it or forget about it, so I wrote. And I wrote. And I wrote. Sunday afternoons were my writing time. After a family lunch, I would go to my room and start. Often it would get to eight or nine at night before I took a breather.

It was the only thing I had ever done that made me get so lost in it that I didn't know or care what time it was or how long I'd been doing it. I loved looking back at the memories, I loved analysing what had happened and what I'd learned from it, and I loved creating—taking words and making them into something entertaining and beautiful (some of the time). I discovered that doing something I loved opened my eyes to see a glimpse of wholeness.

Another time was during my first trip to South Africa. One of the camps I took part in was a weekend for young leaders. We had a busy, fun, fulfilling weekend in the beautiful setting of Oribi Gorge. On the Sunday, just after camp finished, one of the girls stayed behind to talk to me. She had been battling with some issues at home and was eager to talk. She shared her feelings of loneliness with me. She had a good group of friends but was always seen as the strong and happy one, even though that was often the last thing she felt. As she poured out things that she had been dying to say for weeks, I just listened. Saying the right thing hasn't always been my gift, but I can listen. I didn't know what to say, but as I was talking to her, words came out of my mouth that I knew weren't from me. I can't remember now what I said as I comforted and prayed for her, but I knew they were the right words: words that could only have come from God. In that moment, I felt like I was in exactly the right place, exactly where God wanted me to be.

Those moments have been simple. They've been amazing, but even around those times, I have been so aware that there is so much more. So aware that I am broken and empty and have a long way to go to completeness. That makes me think that shalom cannot be fully achieved until we're in heaven.

Sehnsucht is a concept I'm much more familiar with and have always been much more aware of, even though I only discovered last year that there was a name for it. I discovered it through C.S. Lewis, one of my favourite people. I think if old C.S. and I had lived at the same time, we would have been good friends. We're from the same part of Northern Ireland, grew up with the same (slightly random) imaginations, and have the same dislike of English accents.[2] I'm grateful to him for bringing my attention to a word that describes an emotion that I've always thought I was alone in feeling.

Sehnsucht is a German word that doesn't have a direct translation into English. It's usually translated to longing or yearning, but Lewis takes it a bit further than that and describes it as an "inconsolable longing for we know not what."[3] Who you are will determine what it is that produces the longing. For Lewis it was "the smell of bonfire, the sound of wild ducks flying overhead, the title of *The Well at the World's End*, the opening lines of *Kubla Khan*, the morning cobwebs in late summer, or the noise of falling waves."[4]

For me, it's the sight from a plane window as it touches down in Belfast; looking at Jack Vettriano's "Dance me to the end of love;" words from the middle of a Snow Patrol song, "I don't know where to look, my words just break and melt, please just save me from this darkness;" open fires on cold nights; and the vastness of the sea.

The problem with these things is that they cause a longing, but the thing that produces the longing isn't the thing we're longing for; therefore, it can't satisfy the longing.

Sometimes, I find myself just feeling sad for no reason, and I think these are times when something has sparked my sehnsucht. Something beautiful, something tragic, something deep, something that makes me long for a thing that is just out of my grasp. Even in moments of great happiness, the moments when I feel like I'm close to shalom, there is an element of sadness, just a pang, a flicker that tells me this is not all there is.

C.S. Lewis's most popular works must be *The Chronicles of Narnia*, and these books even contain hints of sehnsucht. In the final book, *The Last Battle*[5] (sorry to ruin the end if you haven't read it), the land of Narnia ceases to exist and the characters go to a new world, the "Real Narnia," an allusion to heaven. When they get there, they recognise everything, and they realise that the reason they loved everything so much in the Old Narnia is that it reminded them of the New Narnia (not the other way round).

Heaven is where we are meant to be for eternity, and something deep inside us knows that. Something deep inside of us longs for it even when we don't know what it is we're longing for.

Sehnsucht is what we feel where we are. Shalom is what we *will* feel where we *will* be.

CHAPTER 6

Every new beginning comes from some other beginning's end

. . . on change

> *We have choices: we can choose to embrace change and move forward, or we can choose to let it destroy us. We can choose to abuse change, or we can choose to change the thing that needs to change.*

I LOVE CHANGE.

I love it, I need it, I crave it, and I hope for it. I love the excitement. I love the new things it brings.

And I hate it.

I hate it because of the place where change comes from: a place of discord. I hate it because it hurts, because, even if it is good change, it comes with a cost, with a level of discomfort, with fear.

Change is good, change is necessary, but sometimes . . . well, sometimes it's just plain painful.

Change of job, change of city or country, change of flatmates, change of relationship status. Sometimes, we choose change, but more often than not, it sneaks up on us when we least expect it.

Throughout my life, there have been two extremes in my reaction to change. One has been my complete denial and avoidance of change. The other has been my craving for change for change's sake, which has time and again led to forced and inappropriate change. It has time and again led to my great ability to run away.

Change forced upon us

When I first moved to New Zealand, I had a job lined up in a small physio practice that was part of a much larger chain. I worked there for two years. Over the course of those two years, I came to realise that things needed to change. After two years, I didn't really feel as if I had progressed as a physio. I didn't feel that I was getting any better at my job, and I wasn't particularly being encouraged to get better. I had been given a level of responsibility that was inappropriate for my level of experience and had been given very little support to deal with it. A lot was expected of me, and little was given in return. The job did nothing for my confidence in myself and in my ability as a physiotherapist.

Something had to change.

I was significantly more devoted to my job than my employers were to me. And it was an unhealthy devotion: I worked hard because work was my escape in a way that was becoming less and less healthy. I sort of knew there was something not right and that maybe I should do something about it. I looked at new jobs in the area half-heartedly, knowing ultimately that I probably wouldn't take them because at least I was reasonably secure within the tolerable job I had.

Or that's what I thought.

As it turns out, sometimes when you don't take the chance to make the appropriate change, the chance is presented to you on an unavoidable platter. Sometimes when you refuse to make the change, the change is forced on you.

One Monday morning following a week of work that had been decidedly unpleasant, my boss appeared at the clinic on a day when he wasn't supposed to be there. That Monday was the day he told me that I was going to lose my job; I was being made redundant. I was flooded with emotions: anger that I had been rejected even though I'd given so much to the company; anxiety about what would happen; annoyance with myself that I hadn't left before that; and hurt. I think that was the worst one for me. I had been working through feelings of rejection already, and this felt like a blow to take me back to the place I'd been fighting to get away from. My boss and his family were personal friends, people who had cared for me and helped me adjust to New Zealand life. Although it wasn't their direct decision, I felt rejected by them. And I felt that they could have fought harder for me. My boss told me how difficult it was for him to deliver the news, how he'd stopped the car on the way to work to be sick at the side of the road. But it seemed like lip service. Why would no one advocate for me when I was helpless to do so myself?

So, though I didn't start it rolling, the ball of change was well and truly on its way.

After picking myself up from the initial cloud of emotions, I was thrust into dealing with the change. I sent my CV out to several clinics, researched the options for my work visa, and talked to the management at the rugby club associated with my job to see whether that part of my job would also end. I was very tempted to wallow, but when I started to put one foot in front of the other, God worked, bringing up the openings that perhaps I should've stepped into well before I did.

He provided an ideal job with perfect timing, a job in which I felt wanted, a job with people who were committed to my growth as a physio and supportive of my growth as a person. Physically and practically, God provided for me. Emotionally and spiritually, He worked a miracle in my life and helped me see that there was growth happening and that it would continue to happen.

Change we force

It's usually obvious when things need to change. It's just not always obvious *what* it is that needs to change. I think that fact has been the root of my tendency to run away.

Throughout my teens and early twenties, I was completely restless, unsettled, and unhappy. I had many issues that I knew about, and many that I didn't know about. I knew my life needed a change, but it took a long time for me to get to that place where it could change . . . because I kept changing the wrong thing. When I had a problem, I didn't change myself; I changed my position. When I was having issues with friendships in school, I moved to a different school. When I was having problems with self-esteem and loneliness through university, I ran away to South Africa in the holidays, because it was a place where I hadn't spent enough time to move out of the honeymoon phase. When I was scared of the future after university, scared of who I was becoming, I ran away to New Zealand. (I don't do things on a small scale.)

It was only after 18 months in New Zealand that I finally realised that the change needed to come from inside me, not from what was around me.

Life has been much easier since I realised that.

I have realised that change doesn't always mean growth. We can choose what change means. When things change, when your best friend moves to another city, when your boyfriend breaks up with you, when you lose your job, maybe those things are other people's choices, but we still have a choice to make. We can give up, sit down in the middle of the road, and have a little pity party. Or we can embrace it, keep our eyes looking up, and walk forward.

I'm not underestimating how difficult that is. I know that feeling of not wanting to get out of bed because your heart is so heavy. I know how it feels to cry until you can't breathe properly.

I know how it feels to be unable to cry even though you desperately want to because letting out some emotion has to be better than having it build up inside. But because I know what that feels like, I know I can tell you that it feels so much better when you stop fighting the change and let it mould you. Maybe it doesn't feel better straight away, but down the line, when you realise that you've grown, you'll realise that it's a worthy goal.

There's a line in a song that I played over and over when I was made redundant. The song is "Closing Time" by Semisonic[1] and the line says, "Every new beginning comes from some other beginning's end." So often, change comes out of a place of loss. It may be that it has to. Things that were once new and exciting beginnings come to an end, and that is the tragedy, but the victory is that from that place, new starts come.

I'm a little ashamed to admit how much wisdom I find in *Grey's Anatomy*. It is one of my slightly guilty pleasures. But this is something I learned about change from Meredith Grey:

> Change. We don't like it . . . But we can't stop it from coming. We either adapt to change or we get left behind. It hurts to grow. Anybody who tells you it doesn't is lying. But here's the truth. Sometimes the more things change, the more they stay the same. And sometimes, oh sometimes, change is good. Sometimes change is everything.[2]

CHAPTER 7

Sometimes you know, sometimes you don't

... on God's will

Most of the time, we don't get to see the script before we start acting the movie; on occasion, we may get a hint, but most of the time, we just need to trust the director.

I WISH I ALWAYS KNEW exactly what God had planned for me.

I wish that, before I took each step, I knew that He was smiling because I was about to walk the path He had designed for me.

I wish that, when there were decisions to be made, I knew which one was the right one.

Wouldn't it be a lot easier if God always let us in on the plan? Surely it wouldn't be that much of a hassle for Him to just give us a little hint now and then, just let us know we're going the right way and following the right option. Maybe even a little glimpse of the future: just a two-minute trailer of how life is going to look or a peek at the script!

Sometimes you know ...

There have been times in my life when I've been sure, or as close to sure as I think I'll ever be. Those times haven't come as often as I'd like them to, not nearly as often, but once in a while, they have come. They don't come with absolute certainty, and I'm sure that's just my human nature—I'm always going to doubt and second-guess myself. I'm not even sure that I can describe it; that I can describe how I know that I know.

Only a couple of times in my twenty-something years of living have I felt confident about what I've needed to do, almost inexplicably confident. I think, for me, my work has always represented my security. Typical Western Society—life is about what you do. You go to school, leave school, go to university, get a job, buy a house, etc., etc. It's what's expected, it's the secure path.

The particular job has never been that important to me, but the security definitely has. I've feared that without a secure job, there is too much uncertainty in the future; I could end up having nothing, being nowhere.

Before I moved to New Zealand, if anyone had told me that in two years' time, I would be on the other side of the world from home and would lose my job, I probably wouldn't have boarded the plane. At home, I guess I always thought that if everything went hideously wrong, I could move back home and my family would help me out. That security was removed by being on the other side of the world.

So, when my boss called me into his room that Monday morning to tell me that I was being made redundant, the thing that surprised me most was that, in my flood of emotions, fear didn't top the list.

The hurt, the anger, the shock—those feelings bubbled over and tore at my heart, but among them, there was so little fear. After four weeks' notice, I would have no job. My visa depended on my job, so without a job, it would no longer be legal for me to stay in New Zealand. Did that mean that, after four weeks, I would go back to Northern Ireland? Those were thoughts I had, but as soon as they popped into my head, they seemed to be met with emphatic answers. I don't know how I knew, but I did, I knew that I was meant to stay in

Hamilton, and I knew that if I were, a job, an opportunity, answers would come up.

Nothing pointed to that option. Times were hard for physios all over the place.[1] All around, physios were losing jobs or having their contracts changed. Many physios were moving to Australia, where jobs were more secure and significantly better paid. Friends on both sides of the world began to ask me if I thought that maybe this was God telling me that my time in NZ was over and it was time to go home. It was easy to tell by the way they asked that they thought it was an obvious sign that I should go home. But I knew. Somehow, I knew that Hamilton was where I was meant to be.

I mentioned earlier that God provided the right job in the right time. I sent my CV to about ten physio practices. Only a couple of them got back to me. One of them that did told me that they would be interested in talking to me. So, I went to talk to the practice owner. She told me that they had recently also made someone redundant and that they had no jobs available. I didn't know why she wanted to talk to me, but I left feeling that I had lost nothing.

A couple of days later, the owner called me back, saying that one of her staff members had just handed in her notice, and they therefore had a job opening and would I be interested in applying. I jumped at the opportunity, amazed at the timing of events. I had imagined that I would have to go further afield, to a rural community practice maybe. This clinic was a twenty-minute walk from my house. They were prepared to financially support me for further learning, something I had not been used to. And they offered me a job as a senior physiotherapist, a better job than I had had.

As it all unfolded, I just had to smile, knowing that the feeling of peace that I had came from God. He had it all under control.

That time of assurance was peppered by many of my human doubts but, looking back, I can see that it was rooted in a firm foundation, a reliable foundation, built on a rock. It was a time when I needed assurance, when I risked falling apart without it. And God knows what I need and when I need it. So, sometimes He lets you in on the plan.

... Sometimes you don't

As my friends and I were approaching the end of our four-year physiotherapy degrees, it became very apparent that jobs were scarce. Actually, scarce is an understatement. About seventy of us graduated in my year, and then job hunt began. Unfortunately, most of the previous year's graduates were also unemployed. As a result, for each interview I attended, I knew that about 150 other people were also being sifted through.

I found some part-time jobs that had nothing to do with physio. At one point, I had five jobs[2] that I worked at in varying amounts. It wasn't a very pleasant time of my life. I didn't have a clue what was going to happen. I didn't know if I would find a physio job or if I even wanted one. In the middle of the wondering, I saw an advert in a physio magazine for private practice physios in New Zealand. Although I didn't love physio, there was one part of it that I thought I could be pretty happy in: private practice.

So, I started looking into New Zealand as an option.

I did research: on the country, the physio system, the job potential, flight prices, visas. After talking to the owner of the physio company in NZ, I started looking at the process for getting physio registration.

I did pray. I did ask God was I was supposed to do, whether He wanted me in NZ. I didn't hear a firm answer, so I carried on through the process, figuring that, if it weren't the right thing, a door would close. I would have liked a thunderbolt from heaven, something to tell me that I was doing the right thing—or the wrong thing, if that was the case. Maybe even a little prophetic dream about the future, just something to give me a clue. I didn't get it, so I just carried on.

When I did eventually arrive in NZ, I definitely had a few moments of freaking out, of wondering whether I had actually walked through open doors or if I was just walking through escape hatches. To this day, after being in New Zealand for four years, I don't have absolute assurance that it was the right thing to do. I also don't have a firm knowledge that it was the wrong thing to do.

Sometimes you know, and sometimes you don't.

So what do you do when you don't know? How do you know that you're not just ignoring God's voice? St Augustine of Hippo (I think I would like to be Pip of Hippo; it has a ring to it) said all those years ago, "Love God, and do as you please."[3] When I first heard that, it sounded very flippant to me, but the more I thought about it, the more I saw the wisdom in it. If you live a life of love for God, a life in which you seek to know Him intimately, follow Him closely, serve Him faithfully, if you truly love Him—love in the action sense, not the vague lovey-dovey sense—then what you want to do will be what God wants you to do.

You will know God's will because you will know God.

And maybe it's not always about "right" or "wrong" choices. Maybe it is just about loving God, loving Him wherever you end up, whatever you end up doing.

So, maybe it's okay not to know, not to have all the answers.

Maybe there's a reason why God doesn't show us the trailer before we start playing the movie.

Maybe it's about faith.

Maybe it's about us not being robots.

Maybe if we saw the trailer, we'd run the other way.

Sometimes you don't know, but He always does and maybe . . . maybe that's enough.

CHAPTER 8

In search of the greenest grass

...on running away

Wherever you run to, that's where you'll be.

IT WASN'T UNTIL I'D BEEN in New Zealand for a year and a half that I realised how good I was at running away. Some people do it on small scales: avoiding places or people, changing jobs or schools or churches. Not me. As I said before, I don't do things by halves . . .

. . . so I bought a one-way ticket to the other side of the world.

I made the excuses: there were no jobs in Northern Ireland, I wanted to see a bit of the world, I would probably come back in a year or two, but in reality (even though I wouldn't admit it to anyone, least of all myself), I was getting out.

New Zealand had jobs. New Zealand was desperate for physios . . . New Zealand was very far away.

I had problems that I didn't know how to fix, and I thought and hoped that the grass was greener and the sheep were fluffier on the other side.

After eighteen months in New Zealand, I decided it was time to go home for a visit. I didn't particularly miss it, I wasn't especially homesick, but I had a bit of time and had saved a bit of money, so it seemed like a good idea. Although I wasn't longing for home, I was, without a doubt, unsettled in New Zealand. I was well and truly past the honeymoon stage, the stage when I felt new and different and popular because of that. To everyone around me, I wasn't the "new Irish girl" anymore; I was just Pip, part of the scenery. But I didn't feel like part of the scenery. I didn't feel at home enough for that, so in my mind, I was caught in a strange stage of uncertainty, unrest, and apprehension. I didn't know where I was supposed to be. Should I spend the rest of my life in Hamilton? Or should I just give up on it, renounce it as too difficult, and go back to Belfast? Was there anything for me if I went back? Would there be anything for me if I stayed?

Searching for answers became a big force driving me to return to the homeland, so home I went.

Of course, everyone back home wanted to know all about NZ. They wanted to know what I did, where I lived, who my friends were, what my church was like, did I enjoy living there, did I have plans to come home for good? I gave them the standard answers, the ones I was expected to give, but often I didn't really know the answers myself.

I thank God for friends who aren't scared to be honest.

I had surprised Sharyn one Saturday afternoon. I hadn't told her I was coming home and just showed up on her doorstep. The look on her face was a treat. Definite surprise, but she also looked a bit terrified! We spent a few hours chatting, playing with her new baby, catching up. And she asked me the real questions, not wasting time with the superficial. Did I think I'd done the right thing by leaving? Was it taking me to where I wanted to be? Was it helping me become who I thought I should be? I hadn't kept in contact regularly with Sharyn, so she didn't know a lot of what had been happening in NZ and my thoughts on it.

I answered her questions as well as I could, and she told me what she thought. She told me that she had never thought that going away was the right thing for me to do. I think, initially, I was a bit taken aback and maybe even a little annoyed. Why didn't she tell me that before I went?! But the more I thought about it, the more I realised that I wouldn't have listened to her, I would have brushed it off. It definitely wouldn't have stopped me from leaving but probably would have made me more anxious about it.

I couldn't shake what Sharyn had said and as I thought about it, my eyes began to open. I started to think about the time before I left home when I was deciding what to do, and I saw that I had no great desire to go to New Zealand but a great desire to run to greener grass. I was not happy with my life in Belfast. I had problems with relationships, with jealousy, with doubt, with worry, and I'd tried to get over them. Well, I thought I had. Nothing ever worked. I went to new churches, I tried to sort problems by talking to my friends (or maybe criticising them a bit too much), and I had a few bad experiences with counsellors. Nothing worked, so going somewhere else was my next option, I just didn't realise that was what I was doing.

Or maybe I did realise; maybe I just didn't admit it. Looking back, deep down, I think I did know that I was running away. Nobody very close to me seemed very excited about the idea. Their attitudes were less along the lines of "I'm going to miss you" and more along the lines of "I think you're making a mistake." Most of them didn't vocalize this feeling. Occasionally, they would make comments or ask me if I was sure about it. I guess they knew me better than I thought.

The surprising thing for me was that a similar feeling had been brought up by a new friend in New Zealand. I had lunch with Abby a few days after meeting her at church. Naturally, she asked how I ended up in NZ. I told her about the job situation in NI and how I wasn't fully sure where I was meant to be but that I just kept pushing doors, figuring that if NZ wasn't the right thing, the doors would close. She, in her honesty and realness that I've come to love about her, asked me if I felt like Jonah. Jonah ran away from Nineveh and God's calling, and doors opened for him. He was able to get on the boat. Nothing stopped him from getting on the boat.[1]

It didn't mean it was the right thing.

Over the couple of weeks that I was back home, I was shocked by how many times Sharyn and Abby's thoughts were echoed. Azman, a guy in church whose opinion I greatly respected, who had many prophesies, told me something similar as I spoke to him—he told me that he just had a sense that it wasn't the right thing for me. Again, someone who didn't know me very well, who knew nothing of my issues and the things that I was fighting to avoid, was telling me something that turned out to be a great insight into who I was and what I was doing.

The final hint that I had run away came as I spent time with Cat. Cat was one of the people I was most looking forward to seeing when I got home. Cat and I were close, and I guess it's often the closest friendships that highlight your imperfections. I had always felt that she was better than me in every aspect—prettier, smarter, friendlier, better, better, better. We lived together for three years of university and did many things together, including travelling to South Africa, serving on our Christian Union committee, and working together as physios for a local rugby club. I loved her dearly, and I struggled with her greatly. I knew most of the issues we had were my own, but they came out in anger toward her. The fact that she was more popular made me angry with her. I invented reasons to be annoyed with her and would often give her the cold shoulder. I knew I was doing it, but I didn't know how to stop. And the more I did it, the more frustrated I got with myself and with her. It was, by no means, the first time I had done that in a friendship, but I had no clue as to how to fix it, how to stop myself feeling like I did, and therefore reacting like I did and treating others in that way. So, I ran away from it. I started all over again.

When I went back home and stepped back into what felt like a previous life, I saw how close I was getting to doing the same things in New Zealand. There were a couple of people that I was starting to get close to, and it dawned on me that I was starting to treat them exactly the same way as I had treated Cat. I was starting to get annoyed with them for no reason, was beginning to feel angry and rejected and hurt, when they had done nothing to me.

Being back home, spending time with Cat, I saw it clearly.

When I saw where I had been and where I'd gone, I realised that wherever you run to, that's where you'll be.

I don't think that it's a bad thing to see new places, to go overseas, to move around. The actual act of moving to New Zealand wasn't a wrong thing; it was just my motivation behind it. By running to the other side of the world, I hadn't come close to fixing my problems. If anything, I'd just delayed the process. Changing location does not change who you are. All the issues I had with relationships before I left home—they didn't go away. It just took a little longer to get around to them again.

I realised that nothing was going to change until I stopped running and turned around to face the problem that would chase me until I was too tired to run any more.

Which is why I decided to stay in NZ. You would think (and I think many of my friends at home thought when I was telling them my thought process) that if it wasn't the right thing for me to go to New Zealand, I should leave. But that was most definitely not what I was feeling. It seemed to me that my eyes had been opened by my trip home, but that if I left NZ at that stage, I would be doing exactly what I'd done when I'd left Northern Ireland. I would be running away. So, for probably the first time in my life,

I decided to stay where I was, to turn around and confront issues instead of letting them hound me.

I guess I wondered why, if it had been the wrong thing, why God had let me go to New Zealand, why He didn't just stop me. The answer . . . well, I suppose it's free will. Perhaps He did try to stop me; perhaps I didn't listen. But in those wonderings, I realised more of His love. I realised that He is not a God who would just abandon me because I went a little off course (hmm, even if it was 18,132 km off course). I could see that wherever I ran, God was there first. As far as my problem could chase me, God would chase me more determinedly, more ferociously, more unwaveringly, with more commitment, with more strength and speed, with more desire and single-mindedness. He was there before my problem arose, He was there when it set off in pursuit, and He would be there as I conquered it and long after it was gone.

There is nowhere you or I could run to where God has not already been, where God is not, where He will not be.

CHAPTER 9

Swings, slides and seesaws

... on choices

God has a plan for our lives, but it is not a rigid one, dragging us through its paths without our input. Instead, He invites us to be part of it. He invites us by giving us choices.

I WOULD LOVE TO TELL you that this is a chapter about how to make choices, that I am about to give you a step-by-step guide, maybe even a flow chart to tell you whether you should get a steady job or do some studying or go travelling for a few months; or whether you should go out with this guy or stay single for a while; or whether you should go to university in your own town or move away from home; or whether you should have pizza or pasta for dinner.[1]

I would love to do that, and I wish I could.

I wish I could invent an equation that would tell you (and me) what the right decision is, which decision will turn out best, which option is the one that God is hoping you'll choose. I wish I could tell you where each option will lead, which pros and cons are the important ones, how many people will be blessed or hurt by your decision. I wish I could tell you which is the right one and which is the wrong one. I'm sorry; I can't.

I'm not even going to try. What I am going to do is take it back a step. I simply want to let you know that you have a choice.

You have a choice. You know that? Do you really? Or does God have a rigid plan for you, set in stone, never to be altered? Is the only choice in life whether you're going to obey or disobey God? Or are there choices to be made within the realms of obeying God?

I'm sure Jeremiah 29:11 is one of the most quoted verses in all of history, especially at stages when life is a bit uncertain, when there are decisions to be made.

> "For I know the plans I have for you," declares the LORD, "plans to prosper you and not to harm you, plans to give you hope and a future."[2]

And I am not, in any way, doubting or disregarding that. I fully believe that God knows how my life is going to turn out. I believe He has plans for me, and I believe they are good plans. But I also believe that within those plans, there are choices, and it is not necessarily a case of one being right and one being wrong.

The best way this has ever been explained to me is that it's like a playground. The playground has a fence—a boundary. God gives us space inside that boundary. There is a swing and a slide and a roundabout and a seesaw, and we can choose what we want to play on, as long as we don't go beyond the fence.

The fence isn't God's way of spoiling our fun. Outside of the fence is a place that leads only to pain, doubt, and lostness. Inside the fence, there is love, protection, and wholeness. Maybe there will be hurt (we might fall off the seesaw; I was always a bit scared of those things!), but there will always be someone to pick us up again.

So, maybe God doesn't tell us exactly whom to marry. Maybe He tells us the sort of person we can grow with and form a beautiful life with, but maybe there are a few of those people and maybe, perhaps, possibly, we get to choose who that specific person is. I know so many people who are waiting for flashes of lightning; waiting for God to put a flashing neon arrow above the person they are supposed to marry; waiting for "The One," but what if we actually just get to choose? And there is a bit of risk in that, but I think that if we stay within the boundaries, we won't make a wrong decision. The more important decision is the decision that we're going to commit to love that person, the one we choose.

A few weeks ago, a new job opportunity came up for me. I had been working for about two years in the practice that had been my saviour after being made redundant. Initially, I didn't think too much of the opportunity. I already had a secure job, somewhere that wasn't a bad place to work. I didn't love everything about it and there were a few problems, but what job is perfect? I liked the people I worked with, the business owners had been good to me, and I was comfortable there.

Then I was told about this other job, a job that had many things that I'd wanted but hadn't previously had in a job. It was a bigger practice with a bigger team. It had a very good reputation and was respected in the city. It provided great opportunities and support for professional development, in a direction that I wanted to go. I went to meet with the owner, just for a chat. Even when I took that step, I didn't imagine I would leave my job. The owner was lovely, incredibly understanding, and someone I could really have imagined myself working for. That set off the turmoil. During the week after going to meet with her, a few things happened in my job that began to make me see that I wasn't moving in the same direction as the current bosses wanted the clinic to move in. The turmoil continued . . .

The practice I worked at was small, with three physios. One of the others had just handed in his notice, so I knew that if I left, it would really leave the owners hanging. My boss had been good to me, allowing me flexibility in my work as well as some support, and therefore, I was terrified of hurting her as well as leaving her in the lurch. The whole situation was made even more difficult by the fact that I had to decide by the end of the week and she was overseas, not due to return for another two weeks. I spent a lot of time with a headache that week, weighing up pros and cons. I talked to my family and a few trusted friends to seek advice. I prayed a lot, prayed that God would make it obvious what I should do.

He didn't.

The pros and cons seemed reasonably even overall, and I had no great revelations. So, when it came down to it, I just had to make the decision. It felt as if God was telling me that it was up to me, that He would bless either decision.

I decided to take the new job, but only after talking to my boss. I wanted to do it right. I was aware that she might make me feel guilty, that she might use anything to convince me to stay, out of fear of what would happen if she lost two staff members in a short time. I was dreading it, but I knew I had to do it. We talked on the phone, and she was very gracious. After talking to her, the turmoil calmed, and I felt at peace with the decision.

Finally.

Making the right decision, or at least deciding not to make the wrong decision, can be pretty brain-frying. Sometimes it's obvious but hard, especially when feelings are involved: the decision to do something that might cause others to get hurt; the decision to let something or someone go; the decision to stay; the decision to go.

When there is a decision to be made, God gives us the tools to make it. Sure, the tools don't usually involve flashing neon lights, but instead, He gives us wisdom to know right from wrong. He gives us people that we can trust for advice and be accountable to. He gives us His Word to tell us about His character, His desires, and His plans for our lives.

I've struggled with this whole concept, the thought that we have a choice, with knowing the balance of how much control we have over the choices. God says He has a plan for our lives, so how much choice does that give me? It's easy to go too far one way or the other: to do nothing unless God gives a clear sign about it, or else to do everything unless God sends a lightning bolt to stop you. I guess the key is remembering that God gives us choices within the playground, but the playground still has a boundary. It may seem difficult, but when you know who God is, you will know the boundaries.

I once heard someone say something that has become very profound and significant for me in how I look at life and make decisions about it. He said, "It's not where you go, or even what you do, but who you are when you get there."

The exact decision you make is not the important part, but honouring God in how you make the decision and then deciding to commit to the decision you've made.

CHAPTER 10

Fuzzy feelings and arranged marriage

... on the meaning of love

"I love you" is not just a warm, fuzzy feeling.
"I love you" is a promise.

WE ALL WANT TO BE loved.

It's true; of *course* we all want to be loved...

... but what does that even mean? We all want that warm, fuzzy feeling when someone smiles at us? We all want the security of knowing that we've got some company for the rest of our lives? We all want someone to buy us flowers on Valentine's Day? We all want a hand to hold?

It took me a long time to realise that I didn't know what love was and therefore had no idea of what I was looking for. There were times when I thought I had found it, or at least the potential for it, but I was wrong.

What I've learned is that there's a difference between feeling loved and feeling wanted.

I think, deep down, I've always known that there's a difference, but in the past, I've found it far too easy to deny or ignore that thought. Ignoring all wisdom, all good judgment, I've deliberately gone into situations that I knew weren't right. I've compromised my desire for real love, being motivated by the overwhelming thought, "Surely it's better to be wanted for something superficial than not to be wanted at all."

Maybe I'm not alone in that. If you were honest with yourself, could you see times when you've let yourself or others down because you wanted to be wanted? I'm not judging you for that, not in any way. And I do think there is a reason behind it—it comes from a place that we don't usually want to admit is there, a place formed by hurt, a place that is empty. But what I've seen is that acting out of that motivation leaves you more empty and lost and tired and hurt than before the search began.

There aren't very many of us who haven't had hurts in our lives, hurts that force us into dark corners and lead us to try to heal them our own way. Our own way, the way that feels so good for a moment, then leaves the bitter taste of guilt and dissatisfaction.

Let me give you an example. An example of what I think was the first time that I thought I was in love and thought I was loved. There were so many good things about him. For a start, he was incredibly handsome, especially his eyes. He had tanned skin and dark hair with these amazingly bright, clear blue eyes. And he made me feel beautiful. He would tell me all the time that I was beautiful, and he would say it in a way that I actually believed. He pursued me, he attended to me, and he cared for me. He would go for runs with me even though he hated running. He would drive far out of his way to see me. I almost believed that he would do nearly anything for me.

It was probably about a year before I could really admit all the imperfections in our relationship. I always felt a bit stupid sharing my dreams with him; I didn't know what he would think and was scared that he wouldn't understand or would just think I was silly. We never really talked about God together. We were both insecure. We wanted different things. Although we got on so well on the surface, we didn't connect on any deeper level. Those things would've been major issues, had it gone any further.

But, for just a little while, I truly believed that I was in love with him. Looking back now, a few years down the track, I can see that I was in love with the attention, I was in love with how he made me feel, I was in love with feeling beautiful, even if it was a superficial beauty. It's probably a good thing that circumstances pulled us apart, because I just don't think I would've had the wisdom or willpower to let go of that feeling of being wanted. Ultimately, it ended with hurt. When you call a thing love that is not love, the hurt when it ends can be just as painful as if it really had been love. It can leave you just as broken and confused, maybe even a bit more.

Unfortunately, I could give you about a million examples of times like this, times when my head and heart have been at war. My head tells me about the things that matter, the things I truly believe, while my heart gets caught up in what feels instantly good. There have been so many times when I have confused attention and feeling wanted with love.

Most of us probably know the words in 1 Corinthians 13. We've heard them at numerous weddings, but do we see that they describe the love that is actually what we're looking for?

> Love is patient, love is kind. It does not envy, it does not boast, it is not proud. It does not dishonor others, it is not self-seeking, it is not easily angered, it keeps no record of wrongs. Love does not delight in evil but rejoices with the truth. It always protects, always trusts, always hopes, always perseveres. Love never fails.[1]

"I love you" is abundantly more than "I'm really attracted to you," "I care about you," "I like your company," or even, "I want you." I think *I love you* is a promise. A promise to try, to the best of your ability, to be patient, to show kindness, not to be jealous, not to boast, not to let pride motivate your behaviour toward your loved one. A promise to honour your beloved, to put your beloved first, to keep your temper, and forgive and forget, again and again and again. A promise to grieve with that loved one over injustice and rejoice over freedom and truth. A promise not to doubt but to believe in that one person, to guard that one and never give up on that relationship. A promise to try every way possible not to let your love down.

One of my favourite movies of all time is *Fiddler on the Roof*.[2] (I'm just a complete sucker for musicals.) The story is based around tradition and, in particular, arranged marriages in a small Jewish town in the Ukraine. Tevye and Golde have five daughters, the oldest of whom break away from the tradition of allowing their marriages to be arranged, instead following their hearts into marriages of love. This makes Tevye begin to question if, after 25 years of marriage, his wife loves him, having met her for the first time on their wedding day. It's one of my favourite moments in the movie when they sing, "Do you love me?" Golde is at first confused, wondering why he would ask her such a thing after such a long time, but Tevye persists . . .

Tevye
 But do you love me?
Golde
 Do I love him?
 For twenty-five years I've lived with him
 Fought with him, starved with him
 Twenty-five years my bed is his
 If that's not love, what is?
Tevye
 Then you love me?

Golde
  I suppose I do.
Tevye
  And I suppose I love you too.

I'm not saying that arranged marriage is the way to go (though sometimes I think it would make life a whole lot simpler!), but in Tevye's culture, love was learned. It wasn't a fuzzy feeling; it was action and commitment. The fuzzy feeling came later, and I just think there is something in that. Would the divorce rate be lower if we saw love as something to be worked at instead of a feeling that, if it's not there, should be abandoned? (I'm not making any judgment on people who are divorced. Absolutely not. I know it is, sadly, sometimes the only solution.) All I'm saying is that our generation needs their eyes opened to love—real love.

Maybe it's not what we've thought it was.

CHAPTER 11

"Pongs" about mixed signals

...on flirting

It's the intention that is important.

WHEN ASKING PEOPLE ABOUT THE best examples of flirting they have come across, some of the cheesy pick-up lines have brought on an interesting sensation... never before have I experienced the feeling of wanting to laugh, scream, and vomit all at the same time. I'll share a few of the best with you, and maybe you'll feel it too:

> You wanna know who's amazing and has the cutest smile ever? Read the first word again.
>
> I might as well call you Google, because you have everything that I am looking for.
>
> I hope your day is as radiant as your smile.
>
> Can I take your picture? I want Santa to know exactly what I want for Christmas.

Wow. Just wow. How do people come up with these things? And do they ever actually work??

Those are the obvious examples, but flirting, I'm sure you know, can be significantly more subtle, and when it is, that's when it's dangerous. According to the dictionary, to flirt means "to court triflingly or act amorously without serious intentions;

play at love; coquet."[1] It has been said that flirtation is attention without intention.

We all do it or have all done it at some point. Whether it's been intentional or not, whether it's been successful or not, all of us have let a little sneaky compliment, a little twirl of the hair, a little giggle creep into a conversation, just a little something to let the other person know that we find them attractive, or at least, that we want them to think that we find them attractive.

When someone flirts with you, surely that means they like you, right? So why do they ignore you the next time you see them? Have they changed their mind? Or, did you get it wrong, misread the signs . . . did you just see it differently from how they saw it?

Mixed signals. One minute someone likes you, and then the next minute, he's not interested. How do we avoid mixed signals? How do we deal with them? Is all flirting giving off mixed signals?

I've had many discussions about flirting. I've heard many opinions. I know people who are naturally flirty, without intending to be. They don't even realise they're doing it. I know people who flirt with others in whom they have no interest, merely to get attention. I know people who won't even flirt with someone they do like, for fear of giving confusing signals.

Not to get all "our-generation-has-it-so-hard" or anything like that, but I honestly believe that things have changed with flirting dramatically since the start of texting and Facebook and whatever else. And I don't think the change is for the better. Working out the tone of a text can be one of the most difficult and confusing things and, well, if someone takes your text the wrong way, you can just blame them for getting the tone wrong. It's so easy to hide behind the mask of your cell phone.

I have previously been caught up in cycles of flirting followed by being ignored, then more flirting and more rejection. In these cycles, the way I have been treated has depended on the person's mood. In one of the worst of these cycles, I was spending time with someone I was interested in and initially, I was pretty sure he was interested in me. He texted me regularly, flirting overtly, with not even a hint of subtlety. When he was in the right mood, there would be almost a constant stream of texting. When he wasn't, he wouldn't even text to reply to simple questions. I ended up incredibly confused. So, in my confused state, I wrote a pong about it.

What's a pong, I hear you cry? I'll tell you. Occasionally, when I write, words come out that sort of rhyme and have a vaguely flowing rhythm. I'm definitely not eloquent enough to call myself a poet, so I don't want to call them poems. When I write them, I always imagine that they could be set to music, but I'm no musician, so I can't call them songs. I think they're somewhere in between songs and poems. Therefore, I shall call them pongs. So here it is, "A Pong about Flirting."

> *You turn your head toward my face*
> *My face that's full of hope*
> *You look at me like no one does; then turn away without a pause*
> *And don't care how I'll cope*
>
> *But don't you realise, can't you see*
> *It isn't very fun for me*
> *You raise me up, then run away*
> *So no one's standing there at all*
> *You raise me up, you set the height*
> *The height from which I fall*
>
> *You tell me that it might be love*
> *Someday we'll maybe know*
> *But till that day, we'll laugh and play; but I'll take note of all you say*
> *Then every lie becomes a blow*[2]

Being in that place, it's easy to see why flirting can lead to so much hurt and disappointment. But being at the other end of it, the end where you're getting the attention, the end where you're at the height and haven't fallen yet, well, it's a bit more difficult then.

I have been a physio for a fair few rugby teams in my time. Club teams, age grade representative teams, sevens teams, rugby academies. I've worked with many great rugby players, boys whom I've enjoyed working with, whom I've got on well with. During a campaign, we spend a lot of time together. Usually, there are at least two trainings a week, plus games on the weekends, which may or may not involve long bus trips. It isn't always an ideal place for a single, Christian girl to be, not the ideal circumstances to be surrounded with. And if you want to talk about flirting, well, that's the ideal setting.

I'm going to be honest. It would easy for me not to be, maybe even a bit more acceptable for me not to be honest, but I don't want to tell lies to make myself look good. The flirting has an effect on me. I enjoy it. Not all of it, but definitely some of it. When the boys call me Pippalicious[3], when they tell me they've missed me, when they bring me cups of coffee, it makes me feel good about myself. It makes me feel appreciated, wanted, attractive.

Just last week, we were coming back on the bus after a game, and two of the boys were having a mock fight over me. And I know how ridiculous that sounds, and I know they were just kidding around, but I liked it.

It's so easy to get caught up in it, to start seeking the people and situations that make you feel appealing, but then comes the fall afterwards. Flirting may feel good, but part of the reason I think it does, is that there is the promise of something more. "He wants to flirt with ME, he must like me . . . maybe this could go somewhere." Then my overactive imagination kicks in and before I know it, we're married in my dreams and the next time I see him in real life . . . he doesn't even notice me; he's flirting with someone else; he doesn't care. The more flirting there is, the more I want and the more there is the potential for disappointment. And when that disappointment comes, I fall from the height again, each time a little harder, a little farther.

In some senses, there is nothing wrong with flirting. Well, in some situations. Maybe there's got to be a bit of flirting—how else do you know if someone is interested in you? The problem comes when the flirting isn't followed up, when the flirting is merely for the sake of pumping up an ego or for entertainment. Because then, it is a mixed signal and just leads to confusion, disappointment, and misplaced hope and expectation.

I think the key in all of it is motives. Ask yourself: what do I want out of this conversation? Is it just to boost my ego? What effect is this having on me and the other person? What is it going to leave them thinking about or feeling? Do I want this conversation to go further?

Honesty. It's the key, and sometimes the most important and the most difficult person to be honest with is yourself.

That honesty might not give all the answers, but it's a good start anyway.

CHAPTER 12

Kelly and Hannah

...on personality types

I am not like you, and you are not like him, and he is not like her ... and that's okay. Until we realise how okay it is, we will never live as we are meant to, and we won't allow them to either.

MY FLATMATES, KELLY AND HANNAH, are great. We watch a lot of movies together, eat a lot of food, do a lot of random things (climb trees, get in dryers at the local laundromat—long story), and laugh A LOT. I could've done much worse on the flatmate front.

Kelly and Hannah are incredibly different: polar opposites in many, many, many ways. Some of those differences make them genuinely good friends; other differences make them butt heads a little. Sometimes more than a little.

Kelly is very practical, very friendly, and very organised. If you want someone to organise your New Year's trip or invite you out for lunch after church, Kelly's the one to see. Kelly was the one to bring me home to her family for Christmas to make sure I didn't feel the million miles between my family and me on that day. Kelly loves adventure, loves fun, loves new experiences. Kelly is a great friend and beautiful person.

Hannah is a thinker. Talented, sensitive, a dreamer. When you're not quite sure whom to turn to or where to go and just need someone to sit and pray with you, Hannah is more than happy to be that person. When my heart hurts, Hannah is the one who cries with me. (To be fair, it doesn't take a lot to get Hannah crying.) Hannah loves reflecting, loves beauty, loves pursuing more. Hannah is a great friend and beautiful person.

I think one of the biggest mistakes we can make in life is assuming that everyone is the same, or should be the same. We do it far too easily: assume that everyone thinks and acts the same as us, reacts to things, deals with things in the same way as we do.

We are all different, to varying degrees.

If you Google personality tests, you can find questionnaires that give a name to your personality, based on Myers-Briggs[1], colours, superheroes, and Winnie-the-Pooh. According to the animal test[2], I am an otter. According to the Winnie-the-Pooh test[3], I am Kanga. According to the Disney princess test[4], I am Cinderella. According to the Narnia quiz[5], I am Mr. Beaver (not sure how I feel about this).

It seems like we are fascinated by the different ways that we can describe ourselves. One theory breaks our temperaments[6] down into four fundamental categories, which we can have varying amounts of in our personalities. Broken down into very basic terms, melancholics are sensitive, organised, and creative. Cholerics are strong-willed, confident leaders. Sanguines are passionate optimists who like to make friends. Phlegmatics are laid-back and practical.

I once took a personality test as part of an induction to a committee I was going on for a year. I think it was Myers-Briggs. I think it's significant that I can't remember what test it was because I do remember other key details. I remember where I was sitting in the room. I remember the extroverted person who declared, "no one really wants to be an introvert," and I remember the feeling when the test told me that I was an introvert. Out of a group of about ten, I was the only one. I felt ashamed. To me, introvert meant boring and antisocial, someone who didn't have many friends and who was alone. And I let that eat into me. I let that label define me for a long time. I fought against it. I became determined to prove that I was an extrovert: a cool, funny, friendly person (as I saw it). I clutched that and ultimately tried to make myself into something I was not.

I know I'm not the only one who knows what that feels like. Society, and sometimes even church, almost glorifies what they call sanguines and extroverts without knowing what the terms mean. To be an introverted melancholic, well, that's just unfortunate.

Thankfully, I've come to have a different understanding of what an introvert is. Someone once explained it to me as being less about how you interact with people and more about where you get your energy. Extroverts are most full of energy when they're with people, talking, interacting, at parties, surrounded by others. Introverts can enjoy that and be good at it, but introverts recharge when they're on their own, in their own space.

Once I realised that, life was a whole lot easier. I had been forcing myself to go to parties and be the friendliest person there, but it was exhausting me. I wasn't giving myself time to think, time to be, because I hadn't realised that it was exactly what I needed. I enjoy parties, I enjoy people, but I enjoy them so much more when I've had time to myself as well.

It's one of the things I struggle with about my job, and one of the reasons I've realised that I need to change things. As a physio, I can treat fifteen to twenty people every day. For most of the year, I go straight from work to physio at rugby training, more time with people, and then I spend my Saturdays working at rugby matches. That's a lot of people for an introvert to interact with. And before I understood what I needed, the rest of my life was suffering. I didn't want to hang out with my friends. I had no energy to give to the people I wanted to give it to because I was giving it all to other people.

If I had never accepted that I was an introvert, I would have kept going: constantly surrounding myself with people, constantly forcing myself to be something I am not, and I probably would have burnt out.

That's why I think it's important to understand who you are: not because it seems to be the thing to do these days, not because you should fit into a little box, but because, by understanding who God made you to be and accepting that, you can live in the way He intended you to.

Understanding your personality type can help make sense of how you connect with God. For some people, spending an hour by themselves praying, writing, contemplating, creating is exactly what they need; they finish that hour feeling alive. For others, they would rather chew off their left arm. But for them, they might love to pray with other people; that could be the way they really know God's presence and hear His voice. Others might go out and spend a day chopping firewood to give to people in the community, and in that, know more of God's heart.

We are different and that's okay. In fact, it's more than okay; it's what makes the world turn. If we had a whole world of extroverted sanguines, there would be a lot of smiley people making impulsive decisions. If the world were only made up of introverted melancholics, there would be a lot of creative perfectionists who forget to look around and see other people.

God made us different for a reason, and it's only when we accept that, that we can live as He intended.

I wouldn't change Kelly or Hannah. They are who they are, and I wouldn't want one to be exactly like the other. Their differences are not something to be changed, but something to be celebrated.

CHAPTER 13

From Lynne to David

...on friendship

*A good friendship is powerful,
but a broken one is enough to hold us down.*

LET ME INTRODUCE YOU TO some people, some pretty amazing people, some of the people I love. Some of them are right here in my life every day; some are far away but still very much a part of my life. Some, I haven't seen for many years. All of them have influenced my life. All of them, at one point or another, have been my good friends.

Lynne

Lynne and I have been friends since we were eleven. We met one summer at a church holiday club and kept in touch with letters and phone calls throughout the year. A few times, we joined each other's families on summer holidays. We played tennis together every Saturday.[1] We were at school together for the last two years of high school.

Lynne doesn't like it when people spell her name wrong; that's something we have in common. She buys great gifts. She's good at just about everything she tries, and I don't know one person who dislikes her.

Lynne and I both took gap years in very different parts of Africa. We went to university in different cities. After school, we saw each other maybe only a couple of times a year. Now that I'm in New Zealand, it's much less, but I would still count Lynne as one of my best friends. She's the kind of friend with whom it doesn't matter how long it's been since we were last in touch; we can just pick up where we left off and carry on with the friendship.

Rachel

I called Rachel a friend in high school, but I didn't treat her like one. I'm not sure what it was about her that made me treat her like I did. I found her very annoying, but I think that was more to do with me than her. I would frequently ignore her, frequently be rude to her, and frequently treat her like she wasn't even a human being. She was nothing but nice to me.[2]

Roxy (not her real name)

When my friendship with Roxy started in my early teens, it was a bit of a lifeline for me. I was in a couple of very destructive friendships, and becoming friends with Roxy gave me a way out of that. She made me laugh. She invited me to her church, which was significant in deepening my relationship with God.

I don't remember the turning point, but I do remember the end. She had become controlling, hurtful, too much work, soul-destroying. I didn't know how to deal with it. Instead of being a good friend and talking to her about it, I moved to another school to finish my last two years and cut off contact.

Cat, Julie, Kerryann, Ruthie

These four girls are very different people, and I have very different friendships with each of them, but circumstances grouped us together. We lived together during university. We've had some difficult times and some hilarious times, as well some incredibly random times. Only a tired, late, study-induced conversation could lead us to decide which of us would be which finger if we were a hand (incidentally, I would be the index finger).[3] I love each of these girls as if they were family, and I'm sure that we will be friends no matter where time and circumstances take us.

Di and Mac

Two of my favourite people in the world.

I met them in South Africa when Di started as my boss, but our relationship became so much more as she and her husband, Mac, welcomed me into their home. And not just me. I've never met two people who were so happy when their house was completely filled with people. They would pick me up from the airport when I visited, and they made me a lot of good food and many cups of tea, including me as if I were a family member. They were the kind of people who left everyone feeling better than when they first arrived.

Alice

Alice was my flatmate for about a year and a half. Now we have lunch together when we have the chance; weekly, if it's an option. I find her refreshing: she's honest, blunt when she needs to be. She doesn't shy away from problems and isn't afraid to put herself out there when she needs to. When she asked me to be her bridesmaid, I squealed a little bit, which is very unlike me. I was just so touched to be included in such an important part of her life, and I loved every second of the day.

Kelly

Kelly's a bit of a treat. One of the friendliest and most welcoming people I know, which is a huge blessing when you live on the other side of the world from home. Since knowing Kelly, I've spent every

Christmas with her family, and they have accepted me as part of it. We laugh a lot, eat a lot of chocolate, and share the same love of rugby, Friday night TV, and cats.[4] We are very different people in a variety of ways, but she's one of my best friends.

David

David is a relatively new friend. We've worked together for nearly six months. He's hilarious (which is not always conducive to getting work done). He's honest and straight talking. We have become good friends quickly, and he has been a great support in the past few months. He is one of the few people I can be completely honest and vulnerable with, knowing that he will not judge me, that he will encourage me.

Friendship

Friendship is difficult. And, do you know why it's difficult? Because people are difficult! I've yet to meet a perfect person, someone who is easy to get along with all the time, in every circumstance. And I know for sure that I am not that person.

My friendships, or at least many of my close ones, used to follow a similar course. I would meet someone that I had a lot in common with and form an intense friendship quickly, sharing my heart and soul with them. Then, it was like someone would press a button in my head that started alarm bells ringing for no reason, and I would start to back off. Maybe out of fear that I had shared too much. Maybe because I believed they were better than me. Maybe because I was scared that if I didn't back off first, they would.

For an extreme example of this, I'll introduce you to one more friend, Andrew. Andrew and I both went to South Africa with Scripture Union and as soon as we met, we got on instantly. We had the same sense of humour and the same openness, so in our first week of training in South Africa, where we were far from home and completely out of our comfort zones, we connected and formed a tight friendship. We ended up working in towns an hour apart from each other, and initially, I was hugely excited when Andrew came to visit, but the more he came to visit, the more I backed away. I made all sorts of excuses, but all I saw happening was that I was pushing him away, and I didn't know why. He asked me about it several times. Well, he had to. I was being rude and unfair to him. All my efforts to explain what I was feeling and what I was doing failed, because I didn't even understand why I just didn't like him anymore, why the sight of him made me sink into my angry little cocoon.

We didn't keep in contact much after we left South Africa. I was happy to leave our friendship behind, but something about it kept nagging at me. I just didn't understand why something that had started so positively had become such a mess.

I think I'm a little closer to explaining it now. Friendships are just a really good place for the devil to attack us. It's easy for him because relationships—any kind of relationships that involve two or more people—are never going to be perfect and problem free. People are affected by insecurity, jealousy, anger, unforgiveness, fear, and impatience. As humans, it's easier not to forgive. It's easier not to say sorry. It's easier not to have to admit your faults and open up. It's easier to feel like you're perfect when there aren't people around you to wake you up to the fact that that's nowhere near true.

When you're not surrounded by people, you are much less likely to get hurt. People cannot leave you because they are not there in the first place. You cannot get annoyed or angry with anyone. No one can break promises or let you down. You cannot be jealous, and you do not have to be patient with anyone.

Sounds wonderful, right?

But we are not designed for that. We are designed for friendship, for love, accountability, laughter, giving and receiving support, authenticity. We are designed for growth. We start off rough around the edges. Much of the process of smoothing those edges out comes as the result of relationships and the community we are made to be in.

Without people, we would never learn patience, never know love, never learn how to pick ourselves up after we've been knocked down. We would smile less and laugh less. We would be stagnant, never changing, never developing. People hurt us, but people also heal us.

So, I've learned to value friendships for what they are: good and bad, fulfilling and frustrating, exciting and monotonous, joyful and heartbreaking. I've learned that when people are involved, any people, communication is key. And I've learned that friendships are important, vitally important.

A good friendship is powerful, but a broken one is enough to hold us down.

CHAPTER 14

My cup overflows

... on jealousy and gratitude

Insecurity leads to comparison, leads to jealousy, and the cycle starts again. This vicious cycle can only be broken by gratitude.

I'VE SPENT MUCH OF MY life comparing myself to other people. Not to movie stars or athletes or high achievers as such, but to my friends and acquaintances. When I make a new friend, I'm drawn to them because they're funny or interesting or fun or exciting, but as the friendship goes on, all those things that I initially found so appealing become thorns in my flesh. What starts as my friend being funny or interesting or fun or exciting becomes being funnier than me, more interesting than me, more fun than me, more exciting than me.

"One reason we struggle with insecurity: we're comparing our behind the scenes to everyone else's highlight reel."[1]

It happens all the time—just when I catch myself being grumpy or rude or impatient or treating someone badly, I suddenly become more aware of how friendly and polite and patient and loving my friends are. Then, of course, I begin beating myself up for not being a good person while my friendly, welcoming friend is perfect.

As a rule, we people are pretty good at hiding our worst bits from everyone except ourselves. So, while we are overwhelmed by our inadequacies, the perfect people are dancing around us, flaunting their perfection . . . while secretly beating themselves up for their own imperfections.

I've been in many situations where I've had friends that I naturally spend a lot of time with. In high school, there was Roxy, whose classes were mostly the same as mine and whose church I attended. Later on in school, there was Laura. We liked most of the same things and seemed to get each other in a way that other people didn't really get either of us. In South Africa, there was Shelly. We stayed with the same family, worked together, went to the same church, hung out in the same social circles. At university, there was Cat. We lived together, both studied physio, were on the Christian Union committee, loved South Africa and rugby, and wanted to travel. There was also Kerryann, who also lived with Cat and me and also studied physio. We both played the guitar a little and did a tennis coaching course together. We travelled to Seattle, WA together one year. After a while in New Zealand, there was Kelly. We lived together, went to church together, had the same friends, and did the same job.

These girls have been good friends, great people, but throughout all these friendships (and a number of others), I have had a common issue. I have spent far too long not only comparing myself to each of them, but also believing that everyone around us was also comparing us.

When I look back, I'm not really sure why it mattered so much. Why it mattered that Roxy's clothes were nicer than mine. Why it mattered that Laura was so much smarter than I was. Why it mattered that Shelly was prettier. Why it mattered that Cat could talk to people so much more easily than I ever could. Why it mattered that Kerryann naturally drew people to herself in a way I never could. Why it mattered that Kelly was so much friendlier and more outgoing than I could ever be. But to me, in those times, it mattered hugely.

It mattered so much that it sometimes came close to ruining friendships.

I see now that the root of the issue was largely insecurity. Every time I compared myself to my friends, I came off second best. I was never good enough. I believed I was nothing or, at least, not enough. Never good enough, fun enough, attractive enough, smart enough, talented enough. Sometimes I got close. In school, I always did well, but someone else always did better. Kathryn. For our GCSEs[2], we got the same grades: eight A+'s and an A. We did better than anyone else in our year, and you would think that would have been enough for me. But, no. All I could see was that Kathryn had beaten me in every subject but one: that I was second best. And that wasn't good enough.

Just before my last year of school, Tim, my boyfriend, broke up with me to go out with Laura. She was better than I was.

In South Africa, I could almost guarantee that if I liked a guy, he would like Shelly.

At uni, Kerryann discovered her love of tennis. I had loved tennis for a long time; some might say there was a bit of an obsession there. I liked that I knew a huge amount about tennis and tennis players. I loved Saturday afternoon tennis lessons. It was my thing. When Kerryann started to love my thing, I started to resent it. Instead of embracing it and enjoying having a friend with the same interests, I felt like she was taking over, trying to take my thing away from me, so I stopped doing it as much. I made excuses not to play tennis with her. I tried to outshine her with my tennis knowledge. I think I was terrified that she would become better than I was. I was terrified of her beating me, so I backed away so that she wouldn't get the chance.

Just after uni, Cat and I were the only applicants for the same job. She got it.

That was one of the friendships I nearly ruined. My jealousy was so bad that I struggled to even look Cat in the eye when I talked to her. She went from being someone that I loved spending time with, someone who cared about me enough to stick encouraging notes all round my room when I was having a bad week, someone who shared the same passions as me, to being someone whom I almost resented because every time I was with her, all I could think about was how much more she had than I did, how much more she was, and that it just wasn't fair.

I knew I had a problem with jealousy, but I didn't know what to do about it. As far as I was concerned, it was an emotion I couldn't control. There are some emotions that I've always struggled to grasp. They're almost abstract concepts. My thoughts were: if jealousy is a feeling, how can it be controlled? Like sadness, anger, attraction, you can't make it go away just because someone tells you that you should. Right?

I've come to learn that maybe it's not wrong to feel things like jealousy, but maybe it's more to do with what you do with it. Maybe it was okay, at least normal, for me to feel a pang of jealousy when Cat got the job, but it was definitely not okay for me to ignore her or be rude to her. It was hard not to do those things. Hard, but right.

Things only started to change when I discovered what I think is the antidote for jealousy. I discovered gratitude. Being thankful. Gratitude is a way of taking your eyes off what someone else has and seeing what you have. I knew it for a long time before I started practising it. When I felt jealous, in the worst times, when I actually felt like I was in pain from my lack of what others had, I would say to myself over and over, "My cup overflows, MY cup overflows." At that stage, they were just words. I was so easily blinded. I didn't see the friends I had as blessings, I didn't appreciate my dad, my mum, my sister, and I wouldn't recognise what a gift it was to have the ability and the means to go to university to study a degree that could get me a good career. I expected the gratitude to just descend on me and change my thinking instantly.

I've come to learn that it takes practise. I've learned that doing the action before you feel the emotion eventually helps you feel the emotion. So, I started thanking God. And not just generally, not just, "Thank you for Cat; thank you for my family; thank you for helping me study," but specifics. And I've found that *this* is key. When being thankful, you have to get right into the specifics. "Thank you for that time when Cat plastered my room with encouraging verses, thank you for all the times she's given me lifts even when it's miles out of her way, and thank you for all the brownies that she's made. Thank you that my mum will drive two hours to pick me up from the airport. Thank you for that one really nice patient I had who brightened my day."

It took a little bit of practise and a lot of talking to myself to remind myself of my blessings, but it was pretty amazing how quickly the feeling of gratitude grew and the feeling of jealousy shrank when I started to do what I *would* do if I felt the gratitude and didn't feel the jealousy.

Start with the action; the feeling will come.

CHAPTER 15

No feeling, no hurt

... on apathy

What if you had to choose between a life of mountains and valleys, and a life of flat plains? Which would you choose?

FOR A COUPLE OF YEARS, or maybe a little more, I gave up on feeling.

I'm not sure if it was ever a conscious decision for me or just something that happened, but at some level, I discovered that life was easier when I didn't feel. Emotions hurt; it hurt to care. If I didn't care about people, they couldn't hurt me. If I didn't care about an opportunity, I wouldn't be frustrated by striving for it or disappointed when I didn't get it. If I didn't care about seeking joy and love and purpose, I couldn't be sad when they didn't come.

I remember, as a child, probably when I was eleven or twelve, having the conscious thought that life would be easier if I didn't have people to care about. For a couple of years around that time, I went through what my family called my "Worrying Phase." I don't remember exactly when it started, but I do remember the huge impact it had on me and my immediate family. Basically, when my mum, my dad, or my sister were not in my direct line of sight, I started to panic, to imagine all sorts of things that could happen to them. If my mum was five minutes late to pick me up after school, I was sure she had been in a car crash and died. It started gradually and grew to a crescendo when it got to the stage that if I was out somewhere with my dad and he had to go to the bathroom, I was convinced that someone would attack him, or that he would just disappear. I lost a lot of sleep waiting for my sister, Sarah, to come home when she was out with friends.

It was horrible. I didn't think it would ever end, and I felt completely out of control with a heavy feeling in the pit of my stomach when I was waiting for my family to come. So, I thought it would be easier if I just had no family. I could go shopping in town without having to worry about whether they would show up at the place we were supposed to meet. I could go to a birthday party without spending the last fifteen minutes of the party standing by the window waiting for the car to pull up to pick me up. If I didn't care, if I felt nothing, it would be so much easier.

Maybe that was the start of the apathy, even at that age. If it was, it grew insidiously over the following years, reaching its peak when I was about 22; reaching that peak without my even knowing how I got there. It first hit me in South Africa.

When I first went to South Africa, at the age of eighteen, the family I stayed with lived at the top of Oribi Gorge, which quickly became one of my favourite places in the world. I loved driving home from town through the gorge. Every corner we turned would reveal another view that made me realise that beauty could actually take your breath away. Dramatic rock formations framed by thick bush, giving way to a meandering river at the bottom, and that was just during the day. At night, it was another story. The rocks became looming shadows nestled among a curtain of stars. It was spectacular.

A couple of years after my first visit, when I went back again, driving through the gorge became a means to an end. The scenery didn't excite me. I didn't object to it, I didn't hate it, but it just did nothing to my heart. That was when I realised there was something not quite right.

If it was just about the views, I wouldn't have been that bothered, but that was when I realised that it had been a very long time since anything or anyone had taken my breath away, a very long time since I'd cried, a very long time since I'd felt anything even a little bit extreme.

My friend Lynne once described me as someone who had high highs and low lows. She knew me best in my last two years of high school, when I was going through one of the toughest times I'd ever gone through emotionally. I cried a lot that year, but I also laughed a lot. When I recognised my apathy a few years later, I realised that that had been the last time that I'd had appropriate emotions and reactions to situations.

Since then, there were no high highs or low lows. It was all, well, just average averages.

In the dictionary, there are two definitions for apathy:

1. Lack of enthusiasm or energy; lack of interest in anything, or the absence of any wish to do anything

2. Emotional emptiness; inability to feel normal or passionate human feelings or to respond emotionally[1]

Argh! How easily I can relate to every word of those definitions. I was tired all the time. I didn't want to spend time with friends, I didn't want to go to the movies, and I didn't want to go to the beach for the weekend. I didn't want to do anything. It felt like my emotional dial was stuck on zero. I had managed to rid myself of the extreme negative emotions. I didn't get particularly sad or angry, but the positive emotions were gone too. For someone who used to get excited at the thought of watching the first day of Wimbledon on TV, or a quick phone call to my South African friends, my lack of enthusiasm was shocking.

When you're going through hurt, the kind of hurt that saps your energy, that you feel right down to the deepest parts of your being, the hurt that makes you wonder if it will ever be possible for you not to feel as sore as you are right now, it's so easy to turn off, to fix the hurt by deciding that you won't give it a place. And maybe that's okay, if it's just about the hurt. It's when you take it back a few steps that the problems start.

The cycle of coping and processing becomes warped: you think that if you want to avoid the hurt, maybe you have to avoid the situation, avoid the relationship, and avoid the happiness. If there were no love, there would be no heartbreak. If there were no hope, there would be no disappointment. If you don't have anything, you can't lose anything. You wouldn't have fallen so hard if you hadn't fallen from so high, so maybe the only thing to do is to make sure you never get back up there again, make sure you never feel the good stuff because then you won't feel the bad stuff. Right?

So, what starts as a decision not to feel hurt becomes a process of not feeling anything, but that's okay because feeling hurts. Yes?

Having been there, in that place of not feeling, that place of numbness, I can tell you that it's not a good place to be. I used to watch movies that I thought might make me cry because I would rather cry over something fake than not be able to cry at all. After watching *La Vita è Bella*, *The Lion King*, *Titanic*, *A Walk to Remember*, and *The Notebook*, I gave up, having failed to shed a tear and having become a bit more bitter at over-sentimentalised society. I would daydream about crying on someone's shoulder. I once had a dream in which I was sobbing as a friend hugged me, sobbing uncontrollable tears. I woke up in the middle of the dream with an ache in my tummy. I remember it clearly though it was several years ago.

I discovered that the pattern of feelings I'd developed to try to stop myself from pain was actually worse than the pain itself. Lady Antebellum summed it up for me in a song a couple of years ago; "I'd rather hurt than feel nothing at all."[2] I learned that was true. I got to the stage where I wanted to hurt; I wanted to cry... because losing the highs to spare myself the lows was not worth it.

Yes, there are feelings that we want to block from our hearts: sadness, loss, disappointment, pain, heartache. But is it worth it to also cut ourselves off from the joy, laughter, peace, delight? I've been there, I've come from there, and I can tell you, it's not.

CHAPTER 16

Depression

... on depression

If you're sitting in the dark, and someone shows you where the light switch is, do you stop to say, "If I was a good enough person, I wouldn't need a switch to see the light"?

MY SECOND YEAR OF UNIVERSITY was probably one of the most difficult years in my memory, but it's a little hard to explain why. There weren't any major, disastrous events that made it sad or painful, but it was tough. If I had to describe that year using a colour, it would be grey. Those few months sit under a cloud of nothingness.

Maybe the trigger was when I began to realise I was pursuing a degree that I didn't enjoy and wasn't very good at. First year had been all theory, and I'm fine with theory. Give me twenty quotes and facts to memorize, and I'll have no problem with the exam. I will remember the facts and even put them in a coherent order. Second year started with six weeks of placement, six weeks in a hospital with real patients. I spent my placement in an elderly care unit and, I'll be honest, I was useless. I had been told that it was one of the easiest placements I could do; how hard could walking grannies really be? I knew a few of the previous students who had been there and got high marks: at least in the 80s. After six weeks of doubting myself, my mark of 52% confirmed what I was scared of: I just wasn't a good physio.

I think that was the beginning of it. It set me up for the year, a year when I spent a large proportion of time alone in my room. I was living with good friends, but I shut them out. I didn't allow them to be good friends. I was jealous because they were better physiotherapists; they were better people than I was. I felt boring compared to them. I felt like that's what everyone else thought about me as well. I believed they didn't understand me, that they thought I was just grumpy and attention seeking for no reason, and then I got angry with them for that, unable to see that all those things were in my head.

The whole thought process kept me in my room; it made me retreat even more.

I'm not sure what made me go to see the doctor. It's highly likely that I was there about something else. I'd always been a bit of a hypochondriac, and that year, it completely took over. At different points during the year, I was convinced I had skin cancer, lung cancer, breast cancer, a heart murmur, and anaemia, to name a few. So I spent a lot of time with the doctor. On one visit, I mentioned how I'd been feeling, and the doctor listened before uttering the word that I had been dreading . . . depression. She suggested that she could prescribe anti-depressants, and I quickly shot her down and swiftly left her clinic feeling worse than ever.

I was a Christian; I wasn't supposed to be depressed! Right? To me, it meant that I had failed, that I was doing something wrong. Christians were supposed to rely on God for everything, to be filled with His joy. Nothing bad had ever really happened to me, so what right did I have to be depressed? I pushed it to the back of my head and carried on.

Circumstances continued to be what they were for the rest of that year, but the break over summer was just what I needed. It was refreshing, filled with laughter and freedom. When third year started, things were different from the previous year. I had a good physio placement that made me believe in physio and in myself again. Things around me were better, so it was easier to cope and I was able to ignore the *D* word, reaffirming that I'd been sad about nothing and over-dramatising my life.

It was another four years before I was forced to confront it. Those four years were filled with lots of good things: finishing my degree, a couple of trips back to South Africa, good holidays with good friends, the big move to New Zealand. But beneath all those good times was an undertone that whispered of things that weren't quite right. I was moody. I was apathetic. I lost the ability to cry. I didn't enjoy company yet felt down when I was alone. I knew things weren't right.

At the suggestion and encouragement of a good friend, I started talking to a counsellor, Jan. During my first appointment, I didn't really know what to talk about, but I was amazed at what came out of "I don't know why I'm here but I know I need to be." A couple of months into the counselling, Jan gave me a book to read. It was a book about depression.[1] It was very practical and laid things out very simply. In one chapter, it listed possible symptoms of depression, maybe about twenty of them. I read the list and mentally ticked off all but three or four as things I saw in my life nearly every day at that point. That was my first hint that I needed to sort things out.

It was difficult to go to the doctor. I worked in a medical centre, in the room beside the doctor, so I saw him every day. I picked up enough courage to talk to him and started with some trivial issue. I think I'd had a bit of a sore ear, so I talked about that first. After sorting that out, I took a deep breath and told him my symptoms of depression. He listened, we discussed, and we decided it was the right time to think about treatment for depression. He explained the physiology of it: the imbalance of serotonin and how medication would change that. We talked about my mother and grandmother, who had both been treated for depression, and the decision was made.

I've been treated for depression for about two years now, and taking that step was probably one of the best decisions I've made. No treatment can change my circumstances, but it can help me to react more appropriately to them. It can help me put things in perspective, not to overreact, not to catastrophize, all of which helps me to be a nicer person to be around. It can clear my head. Previously, it felt so difficult to process anything, because I couldn't think of one thing without a million other thoughts and theories and problems flooding into my head. But, when treatment started, it was as if someone turned down the volume button and I could think over the noise.

Maybe I won't have to take anti-depressants forever. Maybe I will. But I know that right now, I have a medical condition that can be treated and that to refuse that treatment or feel guilty about it would be no different from rejecting antibiotics if I had an infection.

I could've called this chapter any number of more appealing, more creative titles. "Feeling Blue," "In the Darkness," "At the Bottom of the Pit" were all possibilities. But I think some things need to be named, and I think the lack of that has often led to the taboo of certain things, especially within the church. It has been hard for me to name it, to allow myself to say it, so I wanted to make sure I didn't carry on that cycle. I wanted to call it what it is, I wanted to say the word because things with names, things that can be defined, are so much easier to fix.

CHAPTER 17

The fingers of a 500-pound gorilla

. . . on pain

I wish pain could be fixed by sunshine and rainbows and kittens instead of honesty and bravery and persistence.

WE SPEND MUCH OF OUR lives trying to avoid pain. We avoid putting our hands in the fire, avoid being hit by a car, avoid the dangerous, sharp, terrifying edge of a piece of paper, especially on our knuckles.

It makes sense to avoid pain.

It is rational and sensible and normal and wise.

It is all those things, but it is just not always possible.

I suppose it is a fact of life . . . at some point, you will hurt. You will trip and sprain your ankle. You will get hit on the head with a rugby ball. You will trap your finger in a car door. Those are usually easy to cope with, easy to get over.

But then there is the emotional pain . . . the pain that hurts your heart. As much as I wish I could say it isn't true, chances are that you will feel the pain of loss. Your heart will be broken. You will suffer from someone else's mistakes. Those hurts, that pain, well, it can make us wish that the only pain we felt was from a broken finger.

As a physiotherapist, I see people in pain every day. Torn knee ligaments, dislocated shoulders, broken elbows, spinal disc bulges, hamstring tears. And everyone responds differently to it. Incidentally, I've found that middle-aged men are generally the worst at coping with pain; one of them once told me I was "a wee slip of a girl, but had the hands of a 500-pound gorilla!"

One of the questions I ask patients at their initial appointment is "on a scale of zero to ten, how bad is your pain? Zero means no pain; ten means the most severe pain possible." Or as one of my friends used to put it, "Zero means no pain, and ten means the pain equivalent to getting a paper cut on your eyeball." (Try saying that without wincing and closing your eyes tight.) It's fascinating to see the variation in answers to this very subjective question. You get some people who come limping in, barely able to touch their bruised and swollen ankle to the ground, and they will tell you that their pain is 6/10 at its worst. Then you get the people who walk in and sit down as normally as anything and tell you that their back pain is a constant 11/10. (I often fight the urge to tell them that this is a physical impossibility; I'm very professional.)

Everybody perceives pain differently and therefore copes with pain differently.

One of the worst things about pain is that it's hard to know how long it's going to last. The majority of my patients will ask me, at some point, how long their injury will take to heal. I can give them the textbook answer, but it's an estimate really. Everyone is different, every human body is different, and every situation is different. I can't predict when my patient might move slightly the wrong way and disrupt the healing of the fibres, restarting the pain, re-opening the wound.

And I think that's what makes it unbearable for some people, maybe more so with emotional pain. When your heart has been broken, I think it would be so much easier to cope with it if somebody told you with certainty, "You'll be devastated for a week, hurt for a fortnight, sad for a month, but then it'll be over." But the fear of not knowing is the worst. After the initial sting wears off, the fear comes from not knowing when the wound will be reopened, when a pang of hurt might take you by surprise.

So we do all we can to stop those pangs, to heal the hurts ourselves.

There is a theory about physical pain called the Gate Control Theory of Pain[1], or the Pain-Gate Theory. In a lot of physio exams through university, there was a fair chance that, if you mentioned the Pain-Gate Theory in your answer, you would get a few marks. The theory is based on knowledge about two types of nerve fibres in our body: pain fibres (which carry signals about pain between the damaged tissue and the brain) and sensory fibres (which carry signals about normal sensation between tissue and the brain). When tissue is damaged, the pain fibres are activated and signals are sent to the brain, telling us we are sore. But if we then rub the sore area of skin (unless it is a giant, gaping wound), the sensory fibres are activated and signals are sent so that we can feel the sensation. The sensory fibres are bigger than the pain fibres, and the theory is, therefore, that when the sensory fibres are activated, their signals override the signals that the pain fibres are sending, and the pain is therefore diminished. It's the reason that your first reaction when you hit your funny bone is to rub your elbow.

It's a reaction that comes naturally. An instinct that just happens in our body's attempt to keep us free of pain. But what if we try to do the same thing with emotional hurts? What if, to stop the pain, we do more stuff: watch more TV, eat more chocolate, work harder, fight more? We do and do and do to try to cut off the signals that the pain fibres are sending. We do anything, anything at all to try to stop the constant reminders that it hurts.

Going back to the physical pain, the thing with the gate control theory is that it takes away the pain when the stimulus is applied, but it does not fix the damage. Rubbing the sore bit lightly doesn't make the torn ligament knit back together; it doesn't heal a broken bone. When the stimulus is removed, the damage remains and the pain starts again.

And how true that is of emotional pain. Eating more cake makes you feel good for a moment, but what about when the cake is gone? Watching another Ryan Gosling movie distracts you for a couple of hours, but when it's over? Doing more exercise keeps you healthy and gives you a sense of accomplishment, but does it really close the wound?

Damage is not fixed by avoiding it or the pain it causes. It is fixed by acknowledging it, admitting that there is something wrong, that it hurts and that something needs to be done about it.

Damage is also not fixed by time. For years, it has been said that time is the greatest healer. My experience does not agree with this. I mean honestly, if something is broken, it's not going to get any less broken just because you ignore it. Yes, injuries can be healed by processes that occur over the course of time, but it is definitely not the *time* that does the healing.

After "when am I going to get better?" one of the next most common things my patients say is "I thought it would just get better over time." They come to see me three months after they've sprained their ankle or had a whiplash, and they wonder why they still have pain. Again, let's pop back to the science. If you tear a ligament in your ankle (as long as it's not a serious complete tear), your body will start to heal it. The fibres of a normal ligament are laid down in an order, a bit like this:

But when your body heals itself, it gets lazy and throws new fibres down in a random order, like this:

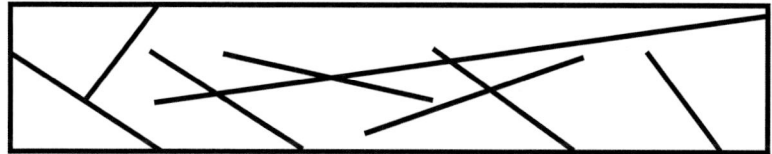

And that's when you get scar tissue, which, although it technically fixes the injury, sometimes causes more problems than the good it does. Scar tissue is weaker than the original tissue, making it more likely to get damaged again. Scar tissue is tighter, less flexible, meaning it doesn't have to go so far before it gets damaged again. The nerves within scar tissue can conduct pain more effectively than normal tissue, meaning more pain.

So it is with emotions over time. If we don't acknowledge and do something about our emotional injuries, the next time something similar happens, our capacity to cope is going to be significantly reduced, and probably will just drive the wound deeper, making it even more difficult to heal.

With this sort of injury, physio treatment is aimed at realigning the tissue fibres, therefore allowing the tissue to heal in an organised way, more similar to the natural way the tissue is supposed to be structured. The treatment hurts. Often, it involves rubbing hard across the damaged area. It's not pleasant! And with emotions, so often, you have to dig up the painful stuff, talk about things that hurt to talk about, confront things that you would rather leave alone.

It hurts. It hurts so much.

But the result has got to be worth it.

Getting to the other side, having healthy tissue and a healthy heart:

> It's difficult, but so is staying in the pain.

CHAPTER 18

Getting over it

. . . on blame

If we insist on stewing in our vat of blame,
we are the only ones who are going to get boiled.

WE'VE ALL GOT ISSUES.

Things have happened to all of us that have made us scared, broken, apathetic, wary. Our parents' divorce, our own divorce, friendships gone sour, failure, disappointment, loss.

And when these things happen, we learn; it is human nature to do so. When someone lets us down, we learn that people can't be trusted. When someone we love leaves or dies, we learn that it hurts to get close to people. When people treat us badly, we learn that we are not worth being treated properly. When people choose others over us, we learn that we are not good enough. When we fail, we learn that trying doesn't always work. When people abuse our vulnerability, we learn that putting up walls leads to less hurt.

I was at a barbecue with some friends last night, and at the end of the night, there were eight of us sitting around the brazier, full of food, looking at the stars, content. We started talking about parents, understanding them and getting to the age when you realise that they're not perfect and they're not invincible. One friend, whose parents divorced when she was in her early teens, said, "It's at about 21 or 22 that you start to understand them, and then you begin to understand your childhood. Then, at about 25, you end up in counselling." We laughed, but looking round the circle, I knew that was accurate for at least half of us.

Often, parents are the first people we get our issues from. How well some of you know that.

Parents who aren't there.

Parents who are overbearing and controlling.

Parents who are selfish.

Parents who take their hurt out on their kids.

Parents who won't let go.

Parents who let go too easily.

Parents who aren't invincible.

Parents who just aren't perfect.

We learn so much from our parents, from basic skills they teach us from day one, to complicated social interactions that we learn through observing and feeling.

Friends aren't perfect either. Teenage friends can be downright flawed and insensitive and cruel. I learned early in my teenage years that people change their minds very quickly. I had a "friend" in high school who had a lot of control over me. We became friends in my second year of high school. In my first year, I had a small group of friends that were very destructive to my heart and my relationship with God. One friend became a way out of that, so I thought she was great. She had been brought up by strict Christian parents so morally, she was someone I looked up to. I wanted to be like her; I admired that she never swore, that she made an effort to talk to people who had no friends, that she wanted to do what was right.

I'm not sure when that all changed.

It was a gradual change, which I think is why it took me a long time to realise our friendship had turned sour. She was my "best friend," a title she claimed as if it gave her some sort of power to treat me even worse than any of her other friends. When you're fourteen, you don't expect your respected best friend to turn into a bully. It started with the little things. She would get annoyed at things I thought were minor; one time she didn't talk to me for a day because I sat beside someone else in English class. I was her "best friend," so apparently I had a responsibility to always sit beside her. Another time, I got the silent treatment for a whole day after not commenting on her new clothes.

Gradually, the silent days became more frequent and the crimes more petty, till I was almost scared to breathe around her. Every day at school, I wished that she would be sick and not come in. I would hide things from her; if I was going to do something with another friend, there was no way I could tell her without being in trouble. Every time it was the same. She would ignore me until I apologised, which I always did because I couldn't bear the silence. In a stage of my life when I was just learning about friendships, it was very confusing. Why would she call me her best friend, yet abuse me with her control? So my heart learned that friendship is fickle; that best friends are only best friends if you do what they want.

Shortly after learning that friendships always involved one friend having power over the other, I learned that I wasn't good enough. Or at least that someone was always better. It was a lesson that seemed to be drummed into me my whole life. I had always been second best. Throughout school, I got the second highest scores. After my GCSEs, I and another girl topped the year, but she just beat me in every subject but one, meaning she walked off with eight prizes at prize giving, and I had none. There was always someone prettier, friendlier, more popular, smarter, funnier, better at sports.

When I was seventeen, I started dating Tim. We had a typical seventeen-year-olds' relationship that lasted four months. It started out a little awkward, had many good moments and many rocky moments, and ended in heartbreak. I confided in him, I told him many things that I had never told anyone else. And he promised never to hurt me.

He promised a promise that no one, especially not a seventeen-year-old, should ever promise

After four months, we broke up. It wasn't a bad break up. Sure, there were tears, but we wanted to stay friends. Which was fine until a few weeks later, when he started dating Laura, my best friend.

When we broke up, I held on. Maintaining a friendship involved having regular deep and meaningful two-hour phone conversations.[1] He told me that he loved me (as a friend) several times after we broke up. I had given him a lot of myself emotionally, and I continued to after we broke up. He was the person who took away my pain and broke down my walls. After we broke up, I was in pain, and I wanted him to take away the pain like he had when we were together. I never realised that I was reinforcing the walls.

They were worried about telling me that they were dating. They knew it would hurt. On the night that they told me, we had been hanging out with a group of friends. Laura took me aside and told me that the thing I feared had come to be, that they never meant for it to happen, that they never wanted to hurt me. All the usual stuff that you're supposed to say in that situation.

I couldn't speak. I didn't know what to do. I didn't cry. Not until they left, anyway. When they did, I cried. Long and hard, I cried. The person who had promised not to hurt me like all those others had, had hurt me a million times more. I had lost him. I had lost her. I had been rejected. I had lost hope. I had nothing. Once again, I was not good enough. And higher and thicker the walls became.

After Tim and Laura, I stewed for months; actually, I guess it was years. I didn't get over it for a long time, because I didn't let myself get over it. I justified so many of my actions by using the hurt I was feeling, which I blamed on them. The whole situation had reinforced my feeling of inadequacy. Once again, I wasn't good enough; someone else was better. Those feelings started to come out as jealousy and, in turn, resentment. Whenever I started to feel as if I wasn't good enough, I would turn that on the person who I felt was better than I perceived myself to be. I started to treat that person with contempt and rudeness, ignoring and complaining to others about that person—I guess trying to drag that one down in the hope of lifting myself up. I believed that since I was the one who had been hurt and needed to be comforted, it was okay for me to treat others however I wanted.

I thought that I would get over it someday. I thought it would just happen. It took me a long time, far too long, to realise that I had to own my issues and that until I did, until I accepted responsibility for my actions, I would never be healed.

People are not perfect.

Realising that was the first step for me. People make mistakes, and mistakes hurt us. But holding onto that hurt doesn't help us; it doesn't even avenge us, as we often wish it would. All it does is eat us up. Taking responsibility for where I was, where I had been, and where I was going had to be the next step. We can't even begin to deal with our issues until we stop looking around for people to blame for them.

It's easy to stew in our vat of blame, to say, "I am like this because of them or him or her, because this happened and because that hurt. It is not my fault."

And yes, I know that it hurt, I know it made you retreat, I know it made you angry and sore and scared, but I also know there is healing, and that healing can't start until you accept responsibility for who you are. And oh, how I wish I had learned that long before I did. How I wish that I had not worn my hurt and anger as a banner across my chest, daring anyone to break through it and fighting them off if they tried.

We can't control them—the parents, the boyfriends, the friends—the people who gave us the issues. But we can control ourselves. We can, and if we want to lead healthy lives, we must.

CHAPTER 19

A new definition

...on missions

Jesus told us to go, but he didn't specify a place for each of us. Some of us will go near; some will go far. Some of us will teach; some will learn. Some of us will go for a long time; some, a shorter time. Some may find answers; some only more questions. But no matter what, Jesus told us to go.

So we must go.

MISSION.

This is a word that means a thousand different things to a thousand different people. Mission statements. Mission organisations. Overseas missions. Diplomatic mission. Space mission. Military mission. Beach mission. Missionary. Even throughout life, its definition has changed for me. *Mission* is a word that has unravelled itself as I've done it and seen it.

When I was fifteen, I had my first exposure to a missions trip—to what was, for me, the definition of mission at that stage. I went with a group of teenagers and three brave leaders to the north of Portugal, around the Oporto area. Not a bad place for a first experience of overseas mission, let's be honest! It seems a long time ago now. I barely recognise the person I was then, but my memories are so clear. I remember the kids' faces we painted at the small town holiday club we helped to run. I remember the feeling of the sweltering heat of the Portuguese summer; I remember wondering how our leaders could drink coffee in that heat (I understand now the need for caffeine). I remember a group of us sitting with a homeless Portuguese man after church, trying to explain a Bible passage to him using broken French because it was the only language we vaguely had in common. I remember the strong taste of the port we had for communion at another church we visited. I remember the fear I felt as I stood on the beach to tell a small crowd some things that God had been speaking to me about.

I couldn't tell you all the ways I changed during those two weeks, but I can tell you, unequivocally, that I did change. I grew up more in that two weeks than I probably had in the previous few years. And it lit a spark in me, a spark that eventually took me to the Philippines, Romania, and South Africa.

By the time I started university, I had spent a month in the Philippines and had just returned from my first seven months in South Africa. And I think it was then that my view of missions started to shift. I was surprised to meet people at uni who seemed almost antagonistic toward overseas missions. Good Christian people, but they just seemed quite against it, which made me examine it a lot more closely. I think, at that time, a lot of university age Christians were spending their summers overseas on missions projects and a lot of people, though supportive of them, felt that there was an enormous amount to do at home, right on our doorsteps. They wondered why, if there was so much to be done at home, they would spend huge amounts of money to go overseas. For a while, I became discouraged by that attitude. It made me question what I had done. I knew that I had done good things in terms of the mission trips I'd been on, but I almost got the feeling that people thought I was either selfish for doing them or just looking for a glorified reason to travel.

While I was at uni, I spent a couple of summers getting involved with missions closer to home. One of them changed my perspective entirely. StreetReach started off small, as an addition to Northern Ireland's biggest Christian festival, a four-day event called Summer Madness.[1] A small group of people involved with Summer Madness took a few days after the 2003 festival, during which they went out to some of the poorer areas of Belfast and served and loved the people of those areas. They cleaned the streets, talked to the people, played with the kids, organised family street parties, worked in people's gardens, and a lot more. StreetReach ran for five years and grew exponentially each year. What started with a handful of people working in the Shankill area of Belfast grew to more than a thousand people working in thirty areas of Belfast. In 2005, I was one of those people. Along with my team, I spent four days working in Tiger's Bay, a strongly Protestant area of Belfast. I lived one train stop away from it at university, but honestly, I had never heard of it. I knew nothing about it, but by the end of the few days, it had turned me around from where I was at that time.

I guess the best way to describe it would be to say that, through StreetReach, God readjusted my perspective on life. It happened just after my second year of university ended. Second year: the year of depression, the year I almost became a recluse, the year I almost dropped out of uni, the year I wondered what on earth I was doing with my life, the year I lost hope. I'm not even sure what it was about StreetReach that so dramatically turned me around. Maybe it was taking my eyes off myself, seeing God at work in a world so close to home yet so far removed from what I knew as home. Maybe it was seeing how people's lives were changed in that community. Maybe it was hearing words of hope spoken over the city. Maybe it was feeling oppression but seeing hope shine a million times brighter.

StreetReach had its last year in 2007, not because it had finished, not because there was no more work to do, but because it saw its goal realised; it saw people inspired to carry on the work on their doorsteps, in their own communities. It ignited a spark that caused wildfire throughout Belfast and even farther afield in Northern Ireland. It made me see that mission didn't always mean getting on a plane and going somewhere where the people spoke another language and ate funny food. Sometimes it simply meant taking the train one stop to show some love to the people just down the road, or next door, or across the street.

I learned a valuable lesson that summer, but none of that convinced me that overseas mission was a selfish or unnecessary thing. If I think about the times in my life when I have changed the most, learned the most, grown the most, those times were when I was in Portugal, the Philippines, South Africa, and Romania.

I'm not saying that overseas missions is all about me, but I also don't think it's solely about the people you help overseas. I think the value to them is huge. People I've worked with overseas have said how much it's benefitted them to have people who care enough to come half way around the world to spend time with them or tell them about God or just play games with their kids or eat a meal with them. But I think the value can grow larger and larger.

What I've found is that overseas missions have given me skills and confidence that I've then been able to use at home to help and encourage people. As a fifteen-year-old, standing on the beach telling people about God, I never would have imagined myself getting up in front of anyone again to talk to them, but as it turned out, in the following years, I was able to give talks in front of kids at camps, my peers at university Christian groups, and in church meetings. As a fifteen-year-old encased in my own sheltered life, I never would have imagined wanting to do a lot for other people.

But overseas, I realised that the world was so much bigger than I was and that I had a responsibility to it.

When I first arrived in South Africa, I NEVER would have imagined I could lead a camp. Six months later, I was doing it. I got to that point through things that forced me out of my comfort zone and gave me the confidence to get there. When I went to Portugal, I never would have thought I would be good enough to lead a similar trip. But I did just that in Romania, and I knew what each of our team members was going through because I had already been through it.

I was recently involved in another mission, this time in New Zealand. There is a small community on the East Coast of New Zealand in the small town of Te Araroa. An organisation in Hamilton approached some people in this community a few years ago to ask if they could bring a group of people out there for a long weekend to serve in the community. The locals said no . . . unless they were prepared to commit to thirty years. They basically said that they didn't want this group coming for a weekend to make themselves feel good, then leaving and going back to normal life. They wanted to form a relationship. So, the project is currently six years into this thirty-year commitment. Every Labour Weekend, a group go to Te Araroa, sleep on the floor of a marae (a traditional Maori meeting house), and serve the community wherever they need to be served. This year, we repainted and reroofed the house of an old man who was sick and couldn't do it for himself.

The approach struck me. Initially, I wasn't quite sure of the point of the thirty-year commitment, until the first evening. Each night, we gathered in the meeting house, and everyone had a chance to talk about where they came from and who they were. In that time, I saw the relationship that had formed and was continuing to be formed, and I saw its value. I thought I understood a lot about mission, but I keep seeing new ways of doing it, new ideas, and new definitions.

I think mission is something we all need to do. I think we should go on an overseas missions trip once in our lives. I think everyone should get involved with serving the community right on their doorstep.

And I think we might need a new definition of mission.

A definition about stepping out of the comfortable bubbles we live in. A definition about exponential growth. A definition about relationship. A definition about living and learning and growing and changing. A definition about serving God and serving people, about changing lives and changing ourselves, about opening doors and opening ourselves.

CHAPTER 20

An Olympic silver medal

... on success and failure

Colossal failures will not come if you don't try.
Monumental successes will not come if you don't fail.

AS I WRITE THIS CHAPTER, the 2012 Olympic gymnastics competition is on in the background (though I may have to turn it off soon; I'm not much of a multi-tasker). It's amazing to watch. The things these people do with their bodies, the strength they have, the flexibility and control; I don't even understand how it's possible. These gymnasts are successful. But how successful? The gold medal winners, you can't really argue with that success. What about the silver? What about the gymnast that comes fifteenth? Not really worth mentioning? But then again, fifteenth out of seven billion people in the world . . .

Yesterday, I watched an interview with Valerie Adams, the New Zealand shot putter who was reigning Olympic champion and was expected to get the gold again. She didn't, missing out to her Belarusian competitor. As she was interviewed, she was fighting back tears. A silver medal . . . and she was devastated. In contrast to that, in the first few days of the Olympics, the New Zealand equestrian event team, which included 56-year-old Mark Todd, won bronze. In a post-match interview, Todd shared his medal with the reporter before joyously lifting her into his arms. A bit different from Adams.

So is success a matter of perspective? Who determines success? How do you become successful? How do you know when you've been successful? What about failure? Is it simply the absence of success?

If you think about successful people, who do you think of? Successful athletes: maybe of Usain Bolt or Michael Jordan or Roger Federer. Successful artists: Leonardo da Vinci or Claude Monet. Successful authors: J.K. Rowling, Jane Austen, John Grisham. Successful businessmen: Bill Gates, Henry Ford, Steve Jobs. What is it that defines their success, puts them in the successful category? Money? Power? Status? Most of us are never going to achieve that level of money, power, or status, or anywhere close to it. What does that mean for us? That we don't need to try because we'll never get there? That we shouldn't strive?

Sorry for all the questions. I just think it's something that we need to ponder more because it's one of those things where the world's opinion is engrained into us, and we don't even realise, so it's important to take a step back and think about what success actually is, what it means to us, and not just what society tells us that it is.

I've been thinking about successful people that I know, and I want to tell you about a couple of the people who popped into my head.

I met Shelly in South Africa. We lived and worked together for six months when we were eighteen. It sometimes amazes me and always makes me smile that, though she was from Zimbabwe and I was from Ireland, we met in South Africa, and a few years later, we somehow both ended up in New Zealand. Shelly and her husband, Ryan, have two beautiful children, three-year-old Emily and one-year-old Tyler. Emily is gorgeous, smart, and friendly. She loves Winnie-the-Pooh and the colour pink. Tyler is one of the smiliest babies I've ever met. He's a cutie. And Shelly is an incredible mother.

I'm not saying she never gets annoyed at the kids or never wants a break or never gets exhausted, but when I see her with them, I see someone who loves her job and, as a result, is very good at it.

Then there's my mum. My dear mama used to be a high school English teacher. She was good at her job. The kids whom she taught liked her. But it wasn't something she was passionate about. It didn't make her come alive. Instead, it sapped a lot of her energy. So, when she was in her fifties, she made some changes. What she had always wanted to do was run a bed & breakfast. And so, she did. I don't think a complete career change is ever easy, but I think it's probably even less so when you've been in the same career for 30 years. But looking at her now, I see her success. She has been running a B&B[1] on the West Coast of Scotland for about eight years. It is a beautiful home with amazing food and fabulously comfortable rooms, and it has achieved a four-star rating from the Scottish tourist board. Most of all, though, I see that my mum is happier than she has ever been—at least, since I can remember.

I don't think that every person needs the platform of a world stage to be successful. I don't think we need to have tangible "things" to show for our success. What I think is that each of us can be successful wherever we've been placed. I love Martin Luther King Jr.'s quote: "If a man is called to be a street sweeper, he should sweep streets even as Michelangelo painted, or Beethoven composed music, or Shakespeare wrote poetry. He should sweep streets so well that all the hosts of heaven and earth will pause to say, here lived a great street sweeper who did his job well."[2]

To me, that is success: doing what you do well, doing what you do to the best of your ability, whatever and wherever it is.

Even in that, there is so much room for failure, another concept that the world has given us a definition of. Is failure merely an absence of success? All those athletes who didn't win the gold medals: did they fail?

One of the rugby players I work with has some decisions to make that may determine the course of his career—whether that career will be a success or a failure. He is 21 and on the verge of breaking into a professional rugby career. The problem is his battle with niggling injuries. An injury he sustained at school kept him out of rugby for two years. It started as a minor injury, but by the end of the season, the damage became much more serious. After a long process of rehab, of trying every avenue to allow him to be pain free, he came back and had a successful representative rugby season. Halfway through the following season, he sustained an injury to his right shoulder. He had just returned to play, when his left shoulder took a hard blow, putting him out for a few more weeks. Added to that were flashes of the return of his old injury.

So, in that, lay the decision: to carry on and make the higher teams, risking further injury and maybe permanent damage. Or to take a season off, risking missing out on rugby development and being overlooked in the future, setting back his career.

He has been getting advice from all sides: coaches who want him to play, family who want him to look after his body, friends who don't understand the burden of injury. There is the pressure of seeing the boys around him succeed and get to where he wanted to be. In the eyes of many around him, his sitting one season out would make him look like a failure. To him, it feels sometimes like his body has let him down.

When I look at him, I see success. I see someone who has learned from his mistakes, someone who uses wisdom to make decisions about his future, someone who is prepared to take a step back in order to propel himself into the future. I'm excited to see where it takes him.

We need to make the distinction between setback and failure, because so often, incredibly often, life deals us blows that knock us ten steps back when we have just fought to take two steps forward. You work yourself sick to show your boss that you are worthy of promotion, only to see your lazy co-worker get that step up. You get up to train at 5 a.m. every morning and get injured the game before the squad is announced. You put aside your insecurities and carefully, wisely invest yourself into a relationship, only to be led on and hurt deeply.

These things are difficult to come back from. They are like a slap to the face that knocks you off your feet and makes you want to cower in the corner, nursing your wounds. The last thing you want to do is get up and try again. But you know what? Being knocked down is not failure. Failure is when you don't get up and try again.

What are the reasons for not trying? I guess the biggest is fear: fear of a setback; fear that when you get up and try again, you're just going to get knocked down once more. When you really want something, when you're fully invested in it, it's so easy to think that not achieving that thing is the end of the world and the end of all hope. Boris Becker's response to his 1987 Wimbledon upset loss to unknown Peter Doohan was one that more sportspeople maybe need to listen to: "I didn't start a war. Nobody died. I just lost a tennis match."[3]

I'm not belittling your problems, not saying that they are not important and don't hurt. I'm just saying that not to try is a bigger tragedy than to be knocked down.

Michael Jordan is probably one of the most successful basketball players in the world. Hugely successful and this is why: "I've missed more than 9000 shots in my career. I've lost almost 300 games. Twenty-six times, I've been trusted to take the game winning shot and missed. I've failed over and over and over again in my life. And that is why I succeed."

Keep going. Don't turn away after missing the shot. Don't give up. Work toward the goal of doing your best at the things that make you come alive. I think those are the keys to success. I'm not the first to say it, and by no means the most eloquent, but I truly believe that the only true failure in life is when you no longer try.

CHAPTER 21

Movie in my mind

... on guarding your heart

*If your fantasy world is what you strive for,
reality is never going to be good enough.*

I HAVE WON WIMBLEDON. A few times, actually. I have been proposed to against the backdrop of many a beautiful sunset. I've had a plethora of successful books published and adored. They've even been made into movies. I've walked down the aisle looking stunning on a number of occasions. I've spoken confidently in front of crowds of avid listeners, sometimes on TV. I've experienced moments of great romance and beauty and success and joy and glory . . .

. . . in my imagination.

And I have no doubt that I'm not the only one. Everyone dreams of those moments: moments of intimacy, adoration, success, pride, promise, hope, and love. Everyone lets their minds wander, whether it's for five minutes before they go to sleep, or in the middle of a lecture, or sitting on the bus. It's not just me, right?

Daydreams, fantasies, imaginings. I've spent a good deal of time indulging in them, ranging from the vaguely possible to the completely outrageous. Sometimes they've been one-off dreams. Other times, they've been ongoing elaborate serial fantasies that have gone on for months, playing like a movie in my mind. When

I was about 16, I would walk to school, which took about 45 minutes. During one period of my life, I spent this time fabricating a story in which I managed to enter the mixed doubles competition at Wimbledon, all the while being part of a romantic adventure with my doubles partner, whom I eventually married after winning the trophy. This dream went on for three months.

For me, nighttime is the worst. I often find it difficult to switch off my brain. As soon as I close my eyes, I go to my fantasy world: the world where I am beautiful and talented and successful and loved. I've tried so hard to stop myself from these thoughts, but it's so difficult with sheer willpower. No sooner have I told myself that I will not think about him than I realise that I'm seeing myself in my wedding dress, reciting vows or imagining what he'll say to me in his speech.

Fantasy, by definition, is imagination unrestricted by reality. It is whatever you want it to be because real life has no bearing on it. It is a world where you are completely in control. You determine the outcome of every situation. You are in charge.

So then, what's wrong with it? Surely, if it's just inside your head, it can't really hurt anyone, right?

The problems come when the lines get blurred, when you expect and hope that fantasy and reality will be the same thing. The problems come when you try to write your own story, when you think that you know best. The problems come when you won't accept anyone or anything that is less than your ideal, less than your fantasy.

I have created people in my mind—not from scratch. Mostly, they're just adjustments to the people I already know. Every time I meet someone I'm attracted to, I create my Mr. Perfect. I take the little I know of him (amazing blue eyes, big biceps, stylish beard) and imagine that he is everything I want. I fantasise about conversations we'll have in which he cares deeply about everything to do with me and understands me like no one else does. But then, I actually start to believe these things are true. Sometimes it has led me to become infatuated with someone I barely know. Sometimes it has caused me to stay in a relationship that I'm not even that happy in because I imagine that he will turn into this person that I have created. Sometimes it has led to frustration and disappointment and heartbreak and hurt and hopelessness, because nobody is perfect.

What about when it's a way of escaping reality? When reality is too much to take? When the things you believe about yourself are too painful so you invent another you: a confident, problem free, desirable you? The problem then is that dreaming it, fantasising about it does not change reality. *Wicked* is one of my favourite musicals, but one of the songs in it breaks my heart just a little, because I understand it so well. Elphaba, the Wicked Witch, with her green skin, is nothing compared to beautiful, blonde, popular Glinda. But Elphaba is in love with Fiyero, Glinda's boyfriend. She sings, "I'm not that girl":

> *Ev'ry so often we long to steal*
> *To the land of what-might-have-been*
> *But that doesn't soften the ache we feel*
> *When reality sets back in...*[1]

The land of what-might-have-been: who doesn't want to spend all their time there? There, where life is exactly as you imagined it. But some time, reality has to set back in, and every time it does, the ache gets that little bit deeper. It seems the only way to make the ache go away is to go back to the land of what-might-have-been until it becomes like a drug. You need more and more and more. You need to spend longer and longer there. The problem is not the dreaming; the problem is using the dreaming to fix an ache that will only be driven deeper by the dreaming.

Proverbs 4:23 says, "Above all else, *guard your heart, for everything you do flows from it.*"[2] Above all else! Above not doing as the wicked do (vs 14), above staying away from corrupt speech (vs 24), above following the way of righteousness (vs 18), above all this, guard your heart. What would make the wise Father give this advice above all else? Could it be that, if you guard your heart, you will stay away from wickedness and corruption? That if you can control the thoughts that you bathe your heart in, you will not want or need to go down those paths to get your contentment and love?

Your heart is where your life comes from, the place that everything you do flows from. Your heart is also where your thoughts, your hopes, your dreams come from.

For most of my life, I've known that it's not good for me to live in this fantasy world, and I've wanted to stop, but usually for the wrong reasons. All the infuriating clichés tell you "when you stop wanting a boyfriend, that's when it'll happen," or "it'll happen when you least expect it." So, I've thought that if I can control my thoughts, when I can stop imagining it happening, that's when it'll happen. But, it's just not enough motivation, or not the right motivation, anyway. Have you ever been really hungry and tried to stop yourself from thinking about food? The more you try to stop yourself thinking about it, the more you find yourself thinking about it. If you do something for the mere physical rewards you will get from it, when those rewards do not come quickly and impatience sets in, where is the motivation for carrying on? It's so easy to slip back into the habit.

So, the reason for getting out of the dream world is not because then all your dreams will come true; it is merely because it will make you a healthier, less broken person. Which must be reward enough.

If we keep living in this place where everything is perfect, the only time we'll be happy, satisfied, or fulfilled will be when we are there. We have to make the choice to live in reality. It may not be that easy, especially when it's a habit we've indulged in for what seems like forever, but the more I go through life, the more I realise that reality is where I live. Reality can be beautiful, but only when I stop trying to make it something that it never will be.

CHAPTER 22

How not to be single

...on singleness

*Don't let being single define you. It's a situation,
not a sentence, just as marriage is a situation, not a solution.*

SOMETIMES I THINK I COULD write a whole book on this subject. Or maybe even a series of books with fifteen volumes and ever-expanding sequels. Most of the time, I wish I couldn't, but as life has had it, I have a fair amount of experience in the art of being single. Thus, I've learned one or two things along the way.

Just to clarify, the title of the chapter is not "how *to not be* single": not a chapter about how to move yourself from singleness to marriedness. That's a chapter I definitely wouldn't do a good job of writing. It's "how *not to be* single": the idea being that much of the time, we don't know how to think or act or how not to think or act when we are single. We seem to spend so much time and energy fighting against it, waiting to get to the "not single" stage, that we don't have a clue how to do this stage.

I'm not saying that I'm good at it or that I'm the model of how to be a perfectly content, fulfilled, inspired, and inspiring single person, but after a bit of practice, I've discovered some things that have made life easier. Here are a few of them:

Don't think there is something wrong with you because you're single.

As I write this, I am in my late twenties and single with no immediate prospects of that changing. That's not always an easy place to be, especially because it seems that it is just not the norm. The majority of my friends of a similar age are married or heading that way.

I have spent many years and great amounts of energy wondering why I am single, wondering what I need to change, wondering what is so repulsive about me, wondering what everyone else has that I do not have.

It only takes a second of taking my eyes off myself and looking around to realise how far off these thoughts are.

I have some amazing single friends. Beautiful friends, smart friends, friends who make me laugh till it hurts, friends who have such interesting stories to tell, caring and selfless friends. I'm not saying they're perfect, but they are pretty awesome. I also have a lot of married friends with the same traits. At the same time, I know some married people who are selfish, rude, scary, cold, grumpy, and socially awkward (again, I also know single people like this).

Just because I am socially not in the same place as lots of my friends does not mean there is something wrong with me.

Same goes for you.

Be aware of the ways you try to satisfy your loneliness.

I may be the queen of looking in the wrong places to satisfy my issues! Usually, we take things that are not, in themselves, bad or wrong. Things like chocolate[1], shopping, going to the gym. For me, it's attention from other people, usually inappropriate people. It's like I know I have a broken and cracked heart and I run from person to person, begging them to fix me. Some of them do. Temporarily. They will say something that makes me feel good about myself, or they'll do something nice for me, or they'll text me when I'm feeling down.

And for an instant, it works.

But not for long.

Be aware that those ways are not the answer.

It's taken me a while to realise this. For a long time, I just pushed and pushed, taking my brokenness to so many people. I looked for that temporary satisfaction however I could get it, because temporary satisfaction was better than facing the brokenness and succumbing to it. But there comes a time when you're forced to face up to your brokenness, and at those times in my life, my eyes have often been opened to see that the things I did to relieve the hurt and loneliness have actually, ultimately, made it a whole lot worse.

Know that relationships,
even marriages, are a situation, not a solution.

Marriage can't fix my problems. I've spent a long, long time believing that it could, believing that if I could just find a husband, if I could be in a long term, committed, healthy relationship, my other problems would go away. Now, I see that's not true. Marriage, though a good and beautiful and remarkable thing, is not the solution to my hurts. I've heard people say that, without doubt, you can still be lonely when you're married. I've also heard married couples say that marriage tends to magnify your problems rather than fix them. What I now know, what I wish I'd known a long time ago, is that I have to sort my problems out myself, with God's help.

A healthy relationship will not fix my problems, but fixing my problems will allow for a healthy relationship.

*Don't feel guilty that the typical
Christian responses, most of the time, don't help.*

"God will bring someone along in His perfect timing."
"God knows what you need better than you do."
"God's love is enough, and it should satisfy you."

These things are absolutely true, and they are usually said by absolutely well-meaning Christians. And they absolutely make me want to scream. I know these things are said to help, to be encouraging, but usually, they just make me feel patronized and like I'm doing something wrong or that they know something about God that I don't. Although these statements are true, the reality of feeling that they are true is a different story. You can't begin to feel they are true just because someone says them to you, so I've found that what was meant to be an encouragement often has the opposite effect.

One of my least favourites is "you'll get it when you stop wanting it so much or when you stop looking for it." Really? REALLY? Who came up with that one? Does that sound like God to you? Is He actually going to wait for us to stop wanting something before He gives it to us? I believed that for a long time, but it's just not logical. God loves us. God delights in us. He delights in giving us every good thing. I know that doesn't explain why you are still single when you want a relationship so much, but I know that it will not happen just because you stop wanting it to. The more I've thought about it and lived life, the more I've come to realise that the time when it happens will not be when you stop expecting it, it will not be when you and God are tight, will not be when you want it less. There is no time, there is no formula. There is nothing we can do to make it hurry up.

Don't feel guilty that you don't want to be single.

If God's love is enough, why do I so badly want to be in a relationship? I've asked myself that question so many times and have usually come up with the answer that my desire to be in a relationship is wrong. I really just need to work a bit harder at being closer to God; then the desire will go away as I become Super Christian who has no desires because God fulfills my every whim and feeling.

I've spent a long time thinking that I was the only person who felt these things, that every other single girl must have a secret that allows her to not care that she is single. I think a lot of girls even feel that. The problem is that we're so scared to admit it, worried that people will judge us because we are unsatisfied, that nobody knows that everyone else is feeling that way too.

We were built for relationship. God put Eve in the garden because He said it was not good for Adam to be alone. I think it's possible to put too much emphasis on relationships, I think it's possible to become obsessed with them, but I don't think that's the case with most of us. Most of us are really just normal.

Don't believe you need someone else to make you whole.

There's a difference between *wanting* a husband or wife and believing that you *need* one. I've spent many years thinking that my life will begin properly when I find a husband, thinking that I can't settle anywhere unless I am in a relationship. I've moved around the world a bit and have wanted to settle, but I think it's always scared me too. What if I settle, and my future husband is somewhere else? I've always been far too willing to move and change and become what other people want me to be in order to not be alone. But what I've learned is that I need to bring my whole self into a relationship if it has any chance of succeeding. I can't expect someone else to complete me. I think the worst mistake we can make is to not live our lives because we don't have someone to live it with. We can't sit around and wait for God's plan to start in our lives. For me, God's best plan started 28 years ago and has kept going through every joy, every heartache, every triumph, every failure, every success, and every fear. His timing has been perfect up till now, in a few ways that I have seen and a million ways that I haven't.

If you are single right now, you need to be okay with that. Not that you stop hoping it will change, but it is where you're at right now; wishing it away, while completely natural, is definitely counter-productive. It's who you are, for now anyway, and who you are is a beloved child of God. No relationship status will ever make that more or less true.

CHAPTER 23

The control of a situation

. . . on peace

Peace does not come from the external, from the circumstances, from contentment and lack of problems. Peace is only real, only lasting when it comes from the internal, a state in our hearts, of which we mostly have no control.

GROWING UP IN NORTHERN IRELAND a few years after the worst of "The Troubles," I heard the word *peace* thrown around a lot. The time leading up to the end of The Troubles, the ceasefire of the main paramilitary groups (like the IRA) is referred to as the Peace Process.[1] In this time, it seemed that peace was something a majority of the Northern Irish people wanted, but with a history of hundreds of years of violence and bloodshed, it was never going to be something that came easily.

Northern Ireland has come a huge distance from where it was in the 1970s, but it isn't there yet. Relative to forty years ago, yes, peace is much more prevalent, but there is still a long way to go to get rid of the hatred, the discord, the disunity.

Peace does not come easily.

If we were given the choice between bombs and silence, between fear and calm, between hatred and love, wouldn't most of us choose the second options, especially when it comes to our hearts and souls?

I find it a bit hard to describe peace when we're talking about peace in our soul. Sometimes it just doesn't seem like a tangible thing; it's a bit abstract. But I've been thinking about times when I have felt what I think is peace. It's funny; one of the first things that pops into my head is a couple of years ago when my job was made redundant. In a foreign country, with the potential of no job and no visa, it's not exactly something that seems very peaceful. But, after getting over the initial shock and fear, a calm settled on me. Everything around me told me that it was not going to be okay, that it was all going to fall apart, but something inside me whispered that it was all going to be all right.

Logically, I guess, looking at it from a human point of view, peace should be present when there is control in a situation, when everything is right in the world, when there is hope and beauty and life and light. That hasn't always been my experience. And I suppose that's why the Bible talks about "peace that passes understanding."² Or in The Message, "Before you know it, a sense of God's wholeness, everything coming together for good, will come and settle you down. It's wonderful what happens when Christ displaces worry at the center of your life."³ Sometimes, we just don't understand why we just feel like it's going to be okay when the chaos around us says it won't.

So if peace is not to do with external circumstances, if it is in fact an internal state of being, how do you get it? How do you even know when you have it? Maybe peace comes from knowing that what you are doing and where you are lines up with what God wants you to be and where He has placed you. I think that if you have questions about those things, about whether you are living in God's will, maybe you need to think about how you feel about where you are and what you're doing. Does it fill you with questions, worries, and doubts that can't be easily defined or answered?

Letting people influence our peace

People easily affect our sense of peace. Sometimes all it takes is a question or a comment from one person to disturb our peace. I remember in the early stages of a relationship when I talked to someone I respected and trusted about the relationship. I was absolutely smitten at the stage, constantly thinking about the guy; I had the cheesy butterflies and everything! Talking to my trusted friend brought me back down to earth a bit and gave me a lot of sensible questions. It disturbed what I thought was peace, but that wasn't a bad thing. Was this relationship going to be a good and positive thing? Was I basing decisions on my feelings of smittenness? Was I falling head over heels into something I hadn't even considered? I needed that turmoil, because I was sitting in a state of false peace. I had lovesickness confused with peace. I needed a little tug just to make sure I wasn't walking into something that would only lead to hurt.

My advice is this: make sure that you only let people you trust disturb your peace. Be very careful about who you let into your peaceful state, because sometimes you need it but sometimes you don't. Sometimes their motives for disturbing your peace are not pure.

Restlessness

Lack of peace is not always a bad thing. Thomas Edison, who invented the light bulb after many failed attempts, said, "Restlessness is discontent and discontent is the first necessity of progress. Show me a thoroughly satisfied man and I will show you a failure."[4] The reason I think restlessness or lack of peace is sometimes a good thing is because of what it stirs in us. If you are sitting in an uncomfortable chair and start to fidget and become restless, the easiest thing to do is to move from the chair and find a more comfortable one where you can relax and be at peace. If you are in a situation where you begin to get uncomfortable and restless, maybe the best thing to do is to move. Maybe a lack of peace can be the biggest motivator.

Something significant happened to me a few years back, just after leaving university. With a degree in physiotherapy but no prospect of a job, I went through several months of purposelessness and restlessness. I was hopping from job to job for six months, at one point working in five different part-time jobs. I was waiting for things to happen that seemed to keep being set back. It was a time of extreme doubt and questioning, wondering if I had a purpose and if I did, what it was. I wondered if anyone, including God, cared. I questioned God's sovereignty. I questioned His plan. I wondered who I was because I based that on what I did. I felt unattractive, unpopular, unwanted, not good enough. I cried out for satisfaction and significance. I pitied myself and complained.

Six months into that time, I reached a stage of peace. I can't remember what started it or if there was even something significant, but I remember that it was as if my eyes and heart were opened. I looked around me and saw people for the first time: people who loved me; people who needed me; people who needed me to bring God to them.

Peace is the only way I can describe this stage. It wasn't contentment or satisfaction as such. It wasn't that I had achieved what I wanted or that I wanted it any less. I guess I just realised that I was okay.

Only a week after I reached this peace, I got a phone call offering me a job. Two days later, I received a letter telling me that an opportunity for which I'd been waiting for months had finally arrived.

The significance came in that it was after I reached the satisfaction and peace, after I made the decision to be positive, that things started happening. I wish I could explain how I got to that place. I wish there was a formula, because I'm sure it won't be the last time

I'm in that situation. But I don't know how I got to that place, and I don't know the way back.

All I know is that it was God then, and it will be again.

CHAPTER 24

Those who pluck the fruits at the wrong time

. . . on patience

It's easy to decide you're going to be patient.
The practise of it is much more demanding.

SHORTLY AFTER I WAS MADE redundant, I worked for a month in a small country town. I vaguely knew a guy from church who lived there, and when he heard that I was working there, he offered to introduce me to the world's best sushi, so one day, we had lunch. The sushi was good, and it was the beginning of a close friendship.

I was very aware of my tendency to fall for just about any boy who showed me some attention, so I'd made up my mind to be careful and not rush anything. As I started to develop feelings, I analysed them cautiously, trying to work out if they were real feelings, or just ones that I wanted to have. Where previously I had been so eager to develop any potential that I had rushed straight in to tell the boy how I felt, this time I waited.

As we discovered that we had a lot in common, we started to spend quite a lot of time together: one week would go watch a rugby match and the next, we would go to see a musical. The week after, maybe a hike, or maybe just chilling with a movie. After a couple of months, I realised that I wasn't making the feelings up;

they were genuine. After a few more months, I realised they were deep. He was different from anyone I had ever liked before. He was the only guy I had ever liked in whom there was no major reason for us not to be together. He had and was most of the things that I could want in a husband, and I was attracted to him for his passion and his morals. I felt that we had enough in common to keep us walking side by side and enough differences to ensure we didn't walk into each other.

After a few more months, the frustration started. I had initially been happy to wait, believing that he would make a move soon. Then "soon" became further and further away. But clearly, so clearly, I heard God tell me to wait, tell me that I was not to be the one to make a move, to start the conversation. If something was going to happen, the guy would have to be the one to make it happen.

In the middle of this, I had a great revelation—glaringly obvious, as the best realisations usually are. I realised that the thing with learning to be patient is that you actually have to *be* patient. I had decided that I was going to be patient, to not take control, to give it to God. I thought that, because I had made that decision, surely things would start happening from then. I didn't realise that there was a long journey ahead in which I would have to make those patient decisions every day.

I started to get confused about the whole situation. We would hang out regularly for a few weeks, text a lot, talk a lot, and then, all of a sudden, I wouldn't hear anything from him for a couple of weeks; then the cycle would begin again. I talked to a couple of friends about it, and that confused me even more because they couldn't understand why I wouldn't just talk to him, which made me question my reasoning as well. It made me wonder if I had heard God wrong or if I was mistaken, but although I couldn't explain why or how, I just knew that God had told me to wait. So I did.

And I kept waiting.

Then, a bit further down the line, things changed. I'm still not absolutely sure what changed them. Maybe it got too intense. I'm not sure. There were two especially intense days that we spent together, that were, perhaps, more like dates than previous hangouts. One evening, we went for a hike up a waterfall to watch the sunset. (Romantic, right?) It was stunning. There have been few things in my life that have taken my breath away, but when I saw the orange sun setting across the green farmland with the sound of gushing water beside us, I didn't breathe for a few seconds. It would have been the perfect place and time to talk about how we felt. But he said nothing. Not even on the way back down. At one point, we crossed a river, and all around us were hundreds of glow worms. It was a clear night, so as we looked up, we could see hundreds of stars as well, so combined with the glow worms, we were in the middle of a sparkling sphere. And still nothing.

A few weeks later, we went to the beach together for a walk and for fish and chips, again at sunset. It started as an amazing day. We sat on a log on the beach and just talked. I knew that I had no one else in my life with whom I felt that comfortable. As we sat on that log, for the first time for probably about a year, I felt like that was the moment. Still, nothing. I said very little as we drove back from the beach. I just didn't understand. We got on so well, we were so at ease with each other; I didn't know why we weren't together.

Following that day, it was another couple of weeks before I heard from him again. The cycle was repeating. And I think that was a turning point. I realised that the disappointment was beginning to affect my life hugely: my mood, my work, my relationships. And I heard a different prompting. I began to see that it was time to talk to him. I don't think God changed His mind about telling me to wait; I think the timing just changed. Whatever it was, I knew that it was time to get control back . . . well, to give it back to God instead of allowing my heart and mind to be controlled by how this person treated me. So, after a lot of God-searching and a little God-fighting, I knew it was time to have the talk.

It wasn't a decision I took lightly, but one Sunday morning after church, I told him that we needed to talk, and we planned to meet that afternoon. I was terrified. I spent the few hours before the appointed time just writing, sometimes weeping, sometimes sobbing loudly. I think I was trying to deal with the disappointment before I even felt it. My heart had become so fragile with all the building up of hope and disappointment. I was scared of what I could lose: his friendship, my confidence. And I was scared of not having the answers to the questions, of not knowing what the previous eighteen months had been all about. I was scared of being back at square one, of feeling more alone, more lost, more pitied and hopeless than ever before. But it was too late to go back, so on I went, limping and cowering, but trusting . . . well, trying.

We met by the river in the shade of a big tree on a sunny day. I was more honest with him than, perhaps, I had ever been. I told him about my confusion, I told him why I felt now was the time to talk. I told him how I felt. And I held my breath till he responded.

One of my biggest fears was that he would have nothing to say, that I had imagined the whole thing, that he had only ever seen me as a friend and I had completely got my wires crossed and would look like a fool. Thankfully, I was wrong about that. It turned out that he had been putting as much hope and prayer into it as I had. He had been wrestling with God, though maybe in a slightly different way than I had. He told me carefully but deliberately that every time he prayed, he felt an unease; it just didn't feel right. He said there had been times when he had been about to drive over to my house and tell me how he felt, but, every time, it just didn't feel right. We talked about it, we said what we needed to say, and I had my answers, mostly.

And I was devastated. After he left, I sat in my car, and I cried and cried and cried, in a way I hadn't cried for months, the kind of crying where you can't breathe, where you hope no one can see you because you know that there's no way you can control yourself if they do. I think that was okay. I think I needed that. I knew there would be a time when I would have to understand, when I would have to pull myself together and carry on with life. But in that moment, on that day, that was my time to cry.

The next day, I went back out to the beach we had been to a few weeks earlier, not to try to relive it all and kid myself with the memories, but because I thought that it should be the place where the healing would start. I spent the day thinking and writing, and gradually, things started to fit into place.

One of my biggest questions was why God had told me to wait when it was just going to end in pain anyway, but I think I know. I think if I had said something sooner, I might have caught him at one of those times when he wanted to tell me how he felt, and he might have set aside his unease, and maybe we would have decided to give a relationship a go. But I think the unease would have come back. We probably would've been happy for a while, but who knows, maybe there would have been even more hurt; maybe we wouldn't even have been talking to each other.

I began to understand, but understanding doesn't stop pain. Often, it explains the pain, to some extent, but it doesn't ease the stabbing hold pain has on our hearts, the hold it had on my heart. I felt crushed. I felt like there was an anvil on my shoulders, pushing me into the ground. It made it a bit harder to do most things, to feel anything but the crushing.

The night we talked was the night of the Rugby World Cup final, when New Zealand won. I watched my favourite sport in a room full of jubilant Kiwis and could barely cheer, could barely smile. I was in a bubble. Everyone around me was in a completely different world, and honestly, I couldn't imagine myself ever again feeling like they did. I couldn't imagine rejoicing.

That was a few months ago, and I have definitely come a long way since then. I still miss him. I fear that we will never get that friendship back. I still don't fully understand what the whole period was about, why we both felt as we did if it's not right for us to be together. I don't understand why I don't feel the same unease as he does. And I don't know what the future holds.

I don't have the happy ending that I thought I would, but I think I have learned. Around the time I started getting frustrated with the whole situation, I was re-reading *The Chronicles of Narnia* (my absolute favourite childhood books). In The *Magician's Nephew*, there was one particular moment that explained to me (perhaps prophetically) why I needed to be patient, why I needed to wait. Talking about the Jadis (who would become the White Witch) after she steals fruit from a magic tree, Aslan says,

> "This is what happens to those who pluck and eat fruits at the wrong time and in the wrong way. The fruit is good, but they loathe it ever after."[1]

I could have taken what I wanted. I could have done things my way, and I do believe it would have been good. But only for a while. Maybe a short while, maybe a bit longer. I know now that the good that could have come from that could not have outweighed the bad that would have resulted for both of us. So maybe I don't have the happy ending that I thought was everything I wanted, but by waiting, who's to say that a far happier ending isn't just around the corner?

Maybe my happy ending isn't what I expected it to be, what I hoped it would be, but who's to say there isn't a better one?

I've always loved to write and dreamed of writing a book. Before I came to New Zealand, in the period when I was working a lot of part-time jobs but had very little security, I wrote a lot and started to get some great opportunities to write. When I moved to New Zealand, the writing was put on the back burner. A couple of times, I tried to get back into it but always found it difficult. I didn't have the time, didn't have the inspiration, and didn't really know what to write. After that conversation when my heart broke, it was like my dormant writer exploded. All of a sudden, I knew how to write again, I knew what to write, and I was motivated to make the time to do it. My writing, once again, had purpose and became a part of who I was. It was just after that point that I started on this book, which has given me more joy and purpose than I ever thought possible. So maybe, just maybe, I had to go through that to get back to my dreams.

I'm not saying that the two things are equal, that writing makes me less lonely or fixes the hurt, but if going through that was what it took to lead me back to things that makes me come alive, then it was worth it. Totally worth it.

CHAPTER 25

First of July

. . . on letting go

> *Letting go is not giving up and admitting defeat; it's choosing to move away from a thing that is defeating you already.*

I LET GO THIS WEEK. Let go of something I have been holding onto for far too long. The guy from the last chapter, the one with whom I had a confusing relationship for eighteen months, the one with whom I believed I could have a godly, successful relationship, the one I believed that I would probably end up marrying . . . well, I let go of him this week.

It's been over six months since we had the conversation. For most of that six months, I've held on, believing that maybe the time isn't now, maybe I just have to hold on a little harder and wait a little longer. Initially, I backed off a bit, not texting as much, not making so much of an effort to see him and spend time with him. But, in my head, I still imagined the day when he would tell me that he was ready now, that he had loved me all along. And that was what I had to let go of: that unfounded hope, that desire to write my own story.

I've known it for a long time, known that I had to let go, but I've done a good job of repressing that knowledge, or at least ignoring it. Turns out, in the end, I was forced to.

About a month back, I heard a rumour. Well, maybe it wasn't even a rumour, maybe more the speculation of a friend, but that speculation was that there could be a spark between my guy and someone else. The second I heard that, something in me snapped. I was at the beach for the weekend with a group of friends, and I escaped to the bedroom and lay on the bed with the light off, hoping no one would notice my absence. I didn't cry, but I just felt like a weight settled in my stomach. It was as if my eyes had been opened at last. I saw how I'd held on to things that I should have let go of, that I was now being forced to let go of.

The unfortunate thing (maybe) was that we had plans for last week, plans that I couldn't go back on. Leading up to Saturday night, I was dreading it a bit, dreading spending the evening with him. But, in some ways, maybe it was good. It gave me an end point. We spent the evening together. It was fine. Just fine. At the end of the evening, I gave him back a couple of his things that I still had and as he left, I exhaled. Finally, finally, I had let go. Not that I had let go of all hope, but I had let go of the hope that there would be love between us.

People may tell you that it feels amazing to let go, that it's refreshing and fulfilling. They're lying. Oh, there are absolutely great things about letting go. There is a freedom in it, and a new hope. But it hurts too. For me, I had believed that I'd done many things as I was meant to. For the first time in my life, I had believed that I had dealt well with a relationship, not rushing it, listening to what God had told me about it, trying my best to obey him. I had believed that by doing that, things would work out as I wanted them to; i.e., that I would get a loving and right relationship out of it. I guess I had believed that I was in control, that if I did those things, I could determine the outcome. So, I had to let go of that belief and accept that I was not in control.

I had to let go of romanticism, of a bit of excitement. Having dinner cooked for me, romantic walks up waterfalls at sunset, having someone to go to when I wanted a bit of company, a bit of care. Those things were tough to let go of because I craved them so much, but I guess I don't actually want those things if there is nothing behind them, if they're not followed up by commitment. Still, they're hard to release.

I had to let go of false hope, looking forward to something that wasn't right. I can still hope for a relationship, for marriage, but I had to let go of hoping for it with him. And those two were quite hard to separate, because, for so long, they were the same thing.

I let go this week, but in a way, I was a bit too late. I was forced to let go. I see now that it would have hurt so much less if I'd done it before I was forced to. It may hurt every nerve in your body to let go, but it hurts so much more when you have to have your hands pried off the thing you're holding on to.

I think I could have saved myself some pain if I had had two key things: honesty and trust.

Firstly, honesty with myself. I'm so good at lying to myself, making myself blind to what I'm doing and what the consequences may be. Maybe I knew that he wasn't right for me, especially in the last few months. And maybe I could have saved myself a lot of hurt if I hadn't ignored the sensible part of myself.

And then, trust. If only this wasn't so hard. Trusting that God will catch you, trusting that He knows your heart, your desires and that He loves you enough to have a perfect plan for you. He's writing a story for you that is so much better than any story you could ever write for yourself.

Sometimes letting go feels like giving up. It's the loss of hope thing. Maybe we just need to see it not as a loss of hope, but as a redirection of hope. Letting go of the hope of getting married to a particular person to hope and trust that there will be someone even better to marry. Letting go of the security of a job that drains you (even if you hope it will give you promotions and money and status) in order to grasp the opportunity of a job that makes you come alive. Letting go of a relationship that you hope will bring love and security but actually tears you down, to have your eyes opened to the hope of a relationship that makes you a better, happier person. Letting go is not giving up and admitting defeat; it's choosing to move away from a thing that is actually defeating you already.

There is a bit of a risk in letting go. What if you do let go of the relationship, and nothing else comes along? What if you decide to quit your job, and you end up unemployed? What if you let go of family security and move to another country and don't make any friends? I wish I could tell you that it will all work out perfectly, that there won't be any loss. I can't, because it is a risk. But I can tell you that if you don't let go of the inferior thing, the better thing will never come around.

I mentioned before one of my favourite lines from a song, from Semisonic's "Closing Time": "Every new beginning comes from some other beginning's end."[1] Sometimes a thing has to end before a new thing can begin. Isaiah 66:9 says, "In the same way I will not cause pain without allowing something new to be born."[2] There may be pain, but from that pain, new birth, new life.

It's always seemed a bit like an abstract concept to me. How do you "let go"? It would be easier if you were actually hanging onto a rope that was dangling into a ravine. Then you could make the physical decision of whether to let go or hang on. But in life, what can you do? For me, there were some physical things I could do. I could stop texting him, not in a rude way, but just not initiating the contact. I could stop seeking opportunities to hang out with him, not avoiding him but not going out of my way to spend time with him. I could stop fantasising about him, guard my heart a little better. This was the most difficult for me, because sometimes I didn't even notice I was doing it until it was too late. So, I'm still working on it, trying to nip the thoughts in the bud before they get out of control and have me walking down an imaginary aisle again.

There is a song by one of my favourite Northern Irish singers, Foy Vance. It's called "First of July." To me, it's a song about letting go.

> *I don't feel particularly good*
> *But don't worry about me, I'll get by*
> *That was the last day of June*
> *This is the first of July*[3]

It doesn't disguise the hurt, but it also proclaims the hope: the hope of turning the page of the calendar, of accepting that it happened, but it is in the past; it was June, and now it's July.

It doesn't feel particularly good. It still hurts, it's still scary to go to that place where you can't see ahead, but you know what? It's so much better than being in the place where you're looking at a future that you've invented for yourself and wondering why it's not happening and when it will.

So this week, this is my first of July.

CHAPTER 26

A god who dangles carrots?

... on hope

My hope is not a blind hope or careless optimism. I can have hope because the One who created hope also created me and loves me.

AHHH, HOPE.

"Hope is a good thing, maybe the best of things, and no good thing ever dies."[1]

So said Andy Dufresne in *The Shawshank Redemption*, one of my favourite movies.

One of the most quoted passages at weddings, 1 Corinthians 13:13 says, "Now these three remain: faith, hope and love."[2] Hope—it's right up there with faith and love, and there's no doubt that they are good things.

Hope is a good thing.

It has to be. The words of great minds, great philosophers, people who have loved and lost and grown and lived, their words suggest that it is hope that got them through, hope that keeps the soul alive. Aristotle said that hope was "a waking dream."[3] John Armstrong (a Scottish physician and poet), in 1744, said that hope was the "balm and lifeblood of the soul."[4] It seems that it's not just a good thing but also a necessary thing.

Why then, does it feel sometimes as if hope is an enemy setting us up for a fall? The more we hope, the higher we get . . . the further we fall, the more it hurts.

We all hope for different things, and the more we want something, the more we hope for it. Whether it's love, success, family, or healing, we all have things that our souls yearn for, even if we don't always admit it. And chances are, if we have deep yearnings in our souls, we've also experienced deep disappointment.

This has been a blank chapter for a while now, one of the last to be started. The thoughts have been going round my head. I've known that I have a lot to write, but I haven't known how to articulate it, or maybe haven't even wanted to. Because sometimes, it's just tiring: the constant highs and lows of hope, having those glimmers, the pain when the glimmers are smashed. This week, the glimmer came back. I have been wrestling and fighting with hope, holding it lightly, wanting to grasp it but begging it not to hurt me again.

It seems that throughout my life, there have been times when I've been close to starting a relationship that has seemed to me to be a good thing, a thing with great potential and it always seems that when I get close to it, it's taken away. There's someone else, or he just doesn't like me enough, or circumstances don't allow it.

The last two years definitely cemented that cycle. With him, the guy from earlier, it was a constant cycle of hope and disappointment. There would be a week or two when we would spend a lot of time together, be in contact nearly every day, and I would begin to hope. I would see the potential, I would believe that finally, finally something would happen, and we would start a relationship. Then, for reasons I didn't understand, he would drop contact. I wouldn't hear from him for a couple of weeks. And my hope would take a blow.

I think it will take a bit of time to recover from that, because you get to the stage where you simply try to repress the hope, because that's better than dealing with the disappointment. So when something that sparks the hope comes along again, you tell yourself all the reasons why it won't happen, all the things that could go wrong.

And oh, how much I've seen that this week. See, there's another guy, a slightly unexpected, surprising one, and I'm beginning to feel things that I haven't felt for an incredibly long time. I've known him for about two and a half years, and I guess I've always found him attractive, but it wasn't until recently that I even thought that he could be an option. So, when it turned out that he felt the same way, the things I should have felt were happiness and hope. And yes, I was happy, but do you know what the absolutely dominant feeling I've had for the last week has been?

Fear.

It's almost overwhelming me. It doesn't help that it's been a week since I've seen him. After we established that we both liked each other last week, he had to go away to work in another town and won't be back for at least another few days. That is not good for my fearful, paranoid, insecure brain.

This could turn into such a good thing, such a good relationship. He could really like me. Maybe it could grow into love. But even writing those words fills me with fear. All week, I've been telling myself that he's lost interest, that he's having doubts, that he doesn't really like me, or at least, not enough. It's been a gloomy week, alone with my anxious thoughts. I think it's a self-preservation thing. I'm so scared to hope, because I know what disappointment feels like. I don't want to go back there. So, I almost sabotage myself, dash my own hopes before anyone else can do it.

Evgeny Baratynsky said, in 1823, "Providence has given human wisdom the choice between two fates: either hope and agitation, or hopelessness and calm."[5] I think hope is a risk. To hope is to risk being disappointed. So, if there is no risk, then there is no reason to be fearful or agitated, because you will not be disappointed.

Proverbs 13:12 says, "Hope deferred makes the heart sick."[6] You know, this week, that's what I feel. I have quashed that glimmer of hope I had last week. I have caused my own hope to be deferred, and heart sick is what I feel. It's a heavy feeling in my chest. It's looking at the sky and only seeing the clouds. It's a sigh and a groan. It's wanting to go to sleep for a really long time. It's wanting comfort from anywhere and getting it from nowhere.

Why, then, is hope so exalted? Why bother hoping when there is so much at stake? Why is hope a good thing? Why does Foy Vance sing, "I guess that's why love hurts and heartache stings and despair is never worse than the despair that death brings . . . Hope deals the hardest blows . . . yet I cannot help myself but hope"[7]? Maybe because of what Samuel Johnson said "Yet it is necessary to hope, though hope should always be deluded, for hope itself is happiness, and its frustrations, however frequent, are yet less dreadful than its extinction."[8]

Having hope is better than not having hope.

A state of hopelessness is a state of apathy.

If we always expect the worst, never dream it will get any better, accept that how we are now is how we will always be, we will never change. We will never work for anything, seek anything, or strive for anything. What's the point? If things aren't going to get any better, why even bother? If we don't hope that cancer can be cured, why bother looking for a cure? If we don't hope that we will make that team, why bother putting in all the training? Without hope, all there is, is giving up.

I guess it's hoping for the right things too. Maybe this is where it's so linked to faith. I really love this quote from Václav Havel, the first president of the Czech Republic. He said, "Hope is definitely not the same thing as optimism. It is not the conviction that something will turn out well, but the certainty that something makes sense, regardless of how it turns out." Isn't that just what we want? We want it to make sense. Yes, I want this potential to turn into something and optimism tells me that it will. But, hope tells me that even if it doesn't, there is a reason, whether it is saving me from unnecessary hurt or saving me for something better.

And I think that what I'm learning this week is that I have something to hope in. My hope is not a blind hope, because my life is in the care of the one who created hope, created me, created the plan for me.

When I take a look back, sometimes it has felt that God has been dangling carrots in front of me. All those times I've gotten close to someone and it hasn't worked out, that is what it has felt like. But what I'm trying to remember is that that's so completely contrary to God's character. The God who "rejoices over me with his song"[10], who loved me so much that He sent his Son to die for me, who forgives me no matter how many times and how badly I mess up, who promises to never leave me or forsake me, of whom it was said "Has He ever promised and not carried it through"[11], that is not a god who will treat me like a play thing, dangling carrots, watching me leap to try to get to the carrots, then pulling them away at the last minute.

No, God is a God who wants to give me a whole field of carrots.

So, my hope is not just wishful thinking; my hope is based on who God is.

And that is why I can still have hope.

CHAPTER 27

Eagles in Zimbabwe

... on beauty

What would the world be like if we were all blind? What if we all saw through the outer surface and our eyes settled on the heart?

I'M NOT SURE WHERE IT came from, but I grew up with the belief that the way I looked was one of the most important things in life. I heard people say that real beauty was within, that personality was the important thing, that looks didn't matter, but I didn't believe it for a second.

My outwardly beautiful friends were the confident ones, the ones who always had boyfriends and friends and success. I never put myself in that category.

I even developed categories of attractiveness. There were the pretty girls: the sweet and unobvious ones who looked good without makeup, without doing anything to their hair, the *Little House on the Prairie* kind of girls who often didn't even realise how attractive they were. On the opposite end of the scale were the hot girls: the ones who knew they turned the boys' heads as they walked past. They could get away with flirting because the boys were under their control. Then there was the ultimate level of attractiveness: the beautiful girls. They had confidence in their beauty, but they didn't need to flaunt it. They had perfect skin, perfect eyes, perfect smiles.

I remember two specific incidents that drove these beliefs home. The belief that there was a thing called beauty and it was all to do with how you looked. And the belief that I did not have it. The incidents themselves may have seemed minor, but they became emblazoned on my brain, so I can remember them even now.

The first happened toward the end of primary school, when I was about ten. Some friends and I were helping the teachers at lunchtime, looking after the younger kids, the four and five-year-olds. One of my so-called friends thought it would be hilarious to encourage one of the little kids to tell me I had a big nose, which this kid did, repeatedly. I remember the steps we were standing on, and I remember the laughter of everyone there. And from that day on, I believed my nose made me ugly.

The other episode happened a few years later. I was finding my way through high school and its challenges, trying to work out who I was, and taking far too many cues from the people around me. Already, I was convinced that all my friends were better looking than I was. Thoroughly convinced. I was away for the weekend with my youth group, during which we were sleeping in a huge dormitory with about twenty other girls. I was lying on my bed reading during some down time. Another girl was reading a magazine on the bed opposite the bed beside mine. She reached an article on facelifts and proceeded to share a bit of it, before looking at me and muttering under her breath, "You could do with one of those." I asked her to repeat what she had said, but she just gave me an innocent smile and said, "Oh, nothing."

Deeper became the belief: I was ugly.

The thing about believing those things about yourself is that you believe them about other people as well. If you place such a high importance on how you look, on how other people see you, then you will do the same to others. As soon as you meet them, you place labels on them, essentially judging them for how thin they are, the colour of their hair, how symmetrical their faces are, what they wear and how well they wear it.

We put people in leagues based on how good-looking they are. I'm ashamed to think how easily this has come to me throughout my life. My friends and I used to talk about couples who were *inter-leaguing*: dating people in higher or lower leagues. Other people describe it as "punching above their weight" when a plain girl ends up with a really attractive guy or vice versa.

We place ourselves in those leagues as well. If it's a low league, we call it humility. "Oh, I'm not good enough to date him; he's far too hot for me." But our opinion of ourselves so easily reflects on how we see other people. If our opinion is that Guy Number One is too attractive for us, what does that say about Guy Number Two, the one we end up with?

I've learned a lot, right or wrong, from *Grey's Anatomy*, and I clearly recall one piercing moment in Season 3.[1] George and Callie got married in Vegas in a snap decision that George later began to regret. Callie began to get jealous of George's best friend, Izzie, of the amount of time he spent with her and the attention he gave her. George couldn't understand this, and in the midst of one fight, he questions her about her aversion to Izzie. She merely states, "Can't you see, George? She likes you!" George replies, "What? No. Don't be silly. She's Izzie. She's blonde and beautiful. No!" As he's speaking, you begin to feel Callie's heart. When her words come, you realise why it hurts. "So what does that make me?"

If we don't stop believing that looks place us in different categories, if we let that thought dominate our opinion of ourselves, and of others, we can't have healthy, functioning relationships.

Grace through sunsets and eagles

Thankfully, through grace, by love, I clearly remember the moment I began to realise that all I had believed was a lie. After navigating my way through high school, driven by other people's opinions of me and of what mattered, the breath of air came in the middle of a broken country in Africa.

The first time I was in South Africa, I took a two-week holiday to go to Zimbabwe with Shelly, the Zimbabwean girl I was living and working with. Her family was about to move to New Zealand, so we went to visit them before they left. As part of the trip, we spent a few days on a houseboat in Lake Kariba, which is one of the most stunning places I've ever seen. We fished, relaxed, read, sunbathed, watched hippos and elephants and crocs, and made the most of an experience that I probably won't have the chance to do again.

Most evenings before it got dark, we would go out on a smaller boat to do a bit of fishing, but one evening, I decided to stay on the houseboat. The whole trip had been a time of rest and reflection for me during a period in my life when everything was changing. That night, I sat on my own at the top of the boat, thinking and praying. The sun was dropping lower and lower on the horizon, turning the sky and the water caramel orange. It reminded me of a picture that had been placed in my head a few years before but that I didn't fully understand at the time. At a time in my life when I was struggling with issues of self-esteem and hurt, I was reading Isaiah 40:31.

> They will soar on wings like eagles;
> they will run and not grow weary;
> they will walk and not be faint.[2]

While reading this verse, I saw a clear picture in my head of an eagle soaring high above a shoreline. It was like I was the eagle, surveying the land I was gliding above. On the shore were long beaches of golden sand bordering an island of palm trees that I could tell held many secrets and mountains begging to be explored. Lapping on the beach were the boundaries of a vast and calm sea, and on the horizon was the sunset in the sky that I could now see around me in Kariba. A giant yellow sphere sinking below the water but colouring the landscape seemed determined to leave its imprint on the world before it left for the night.

I remembered the picture, and I looked around me and thought, "This beauty is God's creation, and He knows it's beautiful. Everything is exactly where He wants it to be, working together in harmony, the way He's always planned for it to be." It took a little nudge before I was able to hear God's voice. "You are my creation. I created you exactly as I want you to be, and you're beautiful. I don't make mistakes!"

That night, I understood for the first time that I was God's masterpiece, that I was beautiful because He made me that way. I still had a lot of wrestling to do to conquer these thoughts that had taken root so deeply in my heart.

It's not something that has come with modern times. We are not the first to put so much emphasis on beauty. In the book of Esther, when the king is choosing a new wife, before the girls were even allowed to see the king, they had to prepare themselves with beauty treatments for twelve months! A whole year of soaking in perfumes and cosmetics. But there is absolutely no mention of their characters, of them doing anything to become more whole, more humble, more honest, more faithful.

And how much is our society like this? How different would things be if we prized humility and patience and generosity and perseverance over a clear complexion and shiny hair? Would there be less depression? Less divorce? Less bullying? Maybe those are big calls, but maybe they are justified.

I think it's time to look deeper than skin deep.

CHAPTER 28

If only you could see yourself as I see you

... on humility

> *Real humility is not putting ourselves down, seeing ourselves as worthless. Real humility is seeing ourselves as God sees us.*

THE WAY WE TREAT OTHERS, the way we interact with them, the way we act in our relationships with them, the way we let them treat us: these things are great measures of the way we feel about ourselves.

I used to wonder why anyone would ever stay in an abusive relationship. Whether it was verbally abusive or physically abusive, why would you stick around? Why not just remove yourself from the abuse? I have known girls who have stayed with boyfriends who have repeatedly cheated on them. Why? I began to wonder a while ago, what if the reason was that they just didn't believe they deserved anything better?

My example of this is a very mild case, and I'm fully aware that there are many a whole lot worse off than I was. When I was dating Tim, he was not abusive, but he also wasn't committed, and I sensed that. I often sensed that, when he was with me, he wanted to be somewhere else, or with someone else. I sensed that he had something, some sort of feelings for my friend Laura. I even verbalised that to a friend once. Surely, knowing that he was pining over someone else was a good enough reason to break up with him. But I didn't.

Eventually, it was Tim who ended it. Why wasn't it me? Maybe I didn't believe I deserved any better. I was prepared to stay with someone who wasn't really that into me because I didn't think I would ever find anyone who was into me.

Believing I deserved better than that was a difficult step.

There are a million reasons for that feeling, and I know I'm absolutely not the only one who's ever felt it. Being rejected by jealous friends, used by selfish boyfriends, abused by controlling parents, ignored by unperceptive teachers: one incident can knock you down; repeated episodes can make it nearly impossible to get up again.

It's far too easy to look for your self-esteem in another person, to base it on a relationship without even realising that is what you're doing. The thing is, no person, no relationship will ever be able to change that feeling in you. In any relationship, of any sort, it's guaranteed that they will, at some point, hurt you, disappoint you, be selfish or jealous, deceive you. And if those are the things that you base your worth on, you are going to live a life believing you are worthless. If you search for your worth, your self-respect in someone else, based on someone else's opinion of you, you will always be disappointed.

The solution? I'm almost a bit wary of suggesting it, because it has been suggested to me so many times, and I have struggled hugely with it. But the solution is to find out and to believe what it is God thinks of you. So many times, I have felt that these are merely words; they have not penetrated the bulletproof shield of self-contempt I've put around myself. Well-meaning Christians have given me verses, which, at times, most times, I've so deeply struggled to believe. Maybe not to believe in my head, but definitely to feel. But these are the things we need to believe, these are the words we need to live by, to let infiltrate deep into our beings, because in them is life.

If we could believe these things, how differently would we see ourselves?

> "The Lord your God is with you, the Mighty Warrior who saves.
> He will take great delight in you; in his love he will no longer rebuke you,
> but will rejoice over you with singing."[1]

When I read this, I see myself as a newborn baby, fast asleep, knowing that nothing can harm me because my father is watching over me. I see a smitten father watching over me, bursting with joy, barely able to contain himself because he is so taken with me. He jumps for joy, sings a happy song, and has a smile that takes over his whole face.

Because of me.

> "No longer will they call you Deserted, or name your land Desolate.
> But you will be called Hephzibah, and your land Beulah;
> for the Lord will take delight in you, and your land will be married."[2]

I've always thought that, if it weren't such an ugly name (sorry to any of you Hephzibahs out there), I would call my first child Hephzibah. Because, even if it is a mouthful, it means "my delight is in her," and I think that is the most beautiful meaning I've heard (this is from someone whose name means "lover of horses"). And because I know that feeling of being deserted and desolate, the thought of being delighted in feels like fresh water on parched lips.

> "See what great love the Father has lavished on us,
> that we should be called children of God!"[3]

I think it's difficult for a lot of people to imagine what it's like to be a child of God. There are so many messed up families in our world. Divorce, neglect, abuse. Families are not now what they were intended to be. So how do you see God as an abundantly loving father when your own experience of a father is one of pain and abandonment? Again, I don't know that I have an answer for that. I can explain how God is so different from humans, but there's a big difference between head knowledge and heart knowledge on this one.

> "Five sparrows are sold for just two pennies, but God doesn't forget a one of them. Even the hairs on your head are counted. So don't be afraid!
> You are worth much more than many sparrows."[4]

I have a couple of really good South African friends whose last name is Sparrow. In one of my meaner moments, thinking I was hilarious, I read them this verse. Thankfully, they took it as a joke. If I ever needed proof that God cares about me, surely this verse is proof—He cares enough to know how many hairs are on my head, although I hope He's not counting the grey one I found yesterday. (Why do I have a grey hair in my twenties?!)

> "For we are God's masterpiece."[5]

God is a God who loves to create. Look at a sunflower, look at a waterfall, look at a giraffe! He loves to create, and He created me. And you. And He is not disappointed with His creation. We are His masterpiece. If He were going to display something in The Louvre, it would be us. That is how proud He is of us, how much He loves us.

I think one of the reasons I've struggled to believe these things is because I've always thought that it was not humble. It seemed to be one of the things teachers hammered into us at Sunday school: it's wrong to be proud; we must be humble. And yes, of course that's a good lesson, but I think I grew up with a bit of a distorted feeling about what humility was. To me, humility was everyone else being better and more important than I was. It was putting myself down. It was not volunteering for things because other people could do them better. It was not admitting when I was good at something or did something well, because that was pride . . .

What I've come to realise is that those self-deprecating attitudes and actions are not humility, and they do not glorify God. Humility is having a real sense of who you are and seeing yourself as God sees you. Seeing the gifts He has given you. Living as His beloved. We are *fearfully and wonderfully made.*[6] Having a proper sense of who we are and who others are and acting out of that, that's the kind of humility God wants.

CHAPTER 29

Confessions of a doormat

... on healthy boundaries

*Deciding not to be a doormat is not an act of selfishness;
it is an act of strength.*

AFTER I HAD BEEN IN New Zealand for a year, two girls from the UK arrived to work for the physio company where I worked. When they arrived, one of them (let's call her Anna) was very confident and had no problem with adjusting and getting to know people. The other (we'll call her Nicki) was shy and tended to get a bit lost in Anna's shadow. I related very easily to that, having spent a lot of my life fighting to find my own identity in the shadow of self-assured friends. So, I wanted to make sure Nicki didn't get left out and had someone that would hear her voice. I told her that, if she ever needed someone to talk to, I knew what it was like to be far away from home and would be there for her.

It started off as I expected. She told me the things she was struggling with; she told me her worries and doubts; she told me that life was difficult. I listened and tried to interject with encouragement when I could. We worked at different branches and so didn't actually see each other that often. Most of our communication was by text, e-mail, or Facebook chat. Looking back, that was probably a large part of the problem. Technology far too often brings the loss of tone and meaning.

I remember the night it began to turn sour.

We were chatting on Facebook, and though I can't remember what we were talking about initially, I do remember the conversation changing. Nicki wanted to know why I was helping her. I think that was her insecurity talking, that she wanted me to tell her it was because she was an amazing person and that she was my best friend. She wanted to believe that I would help her and only her. Any other answer would not be the right one, or a good one. And it was in this that I made my biggest mistake.

Thinking it was a great opportunity to tell her about Jesus and His love, I told her that I wanted to help her because I believed in Jesus, and I believed that it was what He would do and therefore what He would want me to do. I didn't even realise that I was setting myself up in a trap. The conversation continued and gradually became an argument. I was not saying the answer Nicki wanted to hear, so she kept digging for it. No answer I gave was good enough, and I didn't understand why, so I got more and more frustrated. She told me that she had pushed friends away in the past and that she would probably push me away, so I told her that I wouldn't let her push me away. Then she began to question my intentions and whether I would actually be there for her. After a couple of hours (literally), I had to give up. I couldn't think of any more words to convince her, so I told her that I was going to end the conversation for that moment. This, of course, further proved her point that I wouldn't be there for her and that I would just let her down.

Over the next few months, it continued in waves. Nicki would tell me her problems, and I would do my best to be understanding and help where I could. Occasionally, it would be fine. More often than not, it would turn into an argument, and her latest problem would become my fault. Gradually, every conversation became about why I wasn't there for her, why I wouldn't fix her problems, or why I had said that she could talk to me when I clearly didn't mean it. It wore me down, but all I could think was that Jesus would keep going back; Jesus would be a good friend; Jesus wouldn't care that she was taking it all out on him; Jesus would love her anyway.

I believed that I was a bad friend and tried to fix it.

I thought that maybe all I needed was a bit of a break. We were communicating every single day, often several times a day. If she sent me a message that I didn't reply to quickly, she would ask me what was wrong and if I was annoyed at her. It made me feel so annoyed and on edge that I thought if I could just have a few days without it, I'd be much more capable of being there for her.

So I told her, in the nicest way I could, that I had some things I needed to think about and deal with myself, and that I'd really like some time to work on those things. She got annoyed that I wouldn't tell her all of my problems when she had told me all of hers. After some convincing, she agreed that maybe it wouldn't be so bad if she just stopped texting me for a while. I think the longest she managed was about a day, after which, she was very proud of herself for leaving me alone. It continued to escalate, and I sank deeper and deeper into it, believing that I needed to be a good friend, that I needed to be unselfish.

This all happened at a time when I was almost at my breaking point anyway—long before I'd thought of going to counselling but well into the time when I should have been going. I was broken and breaking more each day. I was making poor decisions and had no confidence in my ability as a physio, as a friend, as a person. The more I tried with Nicki, the more I failed. I felt I had failed her and I had failed God, and that pushed me a little further into my pit each time. She noticed my many imperfections and picked holes in them, making me more aware of how terrible a person I was.

After about four months of this, I was exhausted. Every journal entry started with something like, "I can't do this anymore," "I need help," "she's draining life out of me," "I'm so tired," "I have no more words because I have used them all again and again and again."

To give you an idea of the sheer volume of communication, one evening I was watching an episode of *House* in the living room. It was 45 minutes long. I had left my phone charging in my room. At the end of the episode, I went to check it and discovered nine texts from Nicki, starting with a general one, becoming texts about how I never texted her, becoming texts asking what she had done wrong that made me not reply, becoming texts about what a hypocritical person I was. All because I left my phone in my room. Another day at work, she sent me fifty e-mails, that night we spoke for an hour on the phone, and then after the phone call, she texted me ten times.

At times, I would decide (and be advised) to simply not reply, that she would get the hint and give up. I often tried, but she was so clever about what she said. Things like how, by not replying, I was just proving what she'd known all along: that I never really cared and that I was never actually there for her. She told me that she had never believed I could be such a "witch," but she was wrong. My favourite one was the time she texted me to tell me that I should get a t-shirt made that said, "Caution, I turn into a 'witch' unexpectedly!"

There were weekly tutorials at the clinic where she worked, so once a week, I would go over there to learn with Nicki, Anna, and the others. She wouldn't say anything to me during the tutorial, but every single time I would get back to my clinic afterwards, I would have an e-mail from her asking why I couldn't, at least, be civil and say hello to her.

I started to react physically. Every time I got an e-mail from Nicki, my heart would race and I would feel sick. I was getting nosebleeds regularly. I began to lose weight. I felt tired all the time. At the time, I was going to the gym and running a lot, but I found that I could no longer run as far or as fast. I had no energy.

I questioned God over and over. "What are you doing to me with Nicki? Is it a test? Is it a way to make me more patient or tolerant? If it's a test, I keep on failing. It's making me less patient with everyone else because she's draining everything out of me. But I keep coming back to the fact that you would never leave someone who is hurting and lonely like she is. But she's killing my soul. She's making it harder to get up in the mornings and sleep at night and get through the day . . . how can I even read my Bible when I've just told her to leave me alone?"

She made me scared to befriend anyone again. She told me once that if anyone else new ever came to work for our company, that I shouldn't ever offer to be there for them. I always thought that my desire and ability to make friends and to see when people might need a friend was a positive quality I had. At that stage, I thought it was almost the only positive quality I had. And when she told me that, I crossed it off the very short list.

And then she found what was one of my deepest fears and issues. On the 11th of January, almost a year after she had arrived in the country, she told me that I was not the same person I was when she and Anna had first arrived. She was not to know how deep that cut. A couple of other significant people, including Tim, my first boyfriend, had told me similar things in the previous few years, not necessarily in a nasty context, but I had been told that I'd changed. In my broken and confused heart, I saw it as them saying that the more they got to know me, the less they liked me. Nicki hit that nail deeper into my heart.

The issue became even more serious when the threats began: she was going to leave work because she couldn't work with someone who couldn't even reply to her texts. She was going to go back to the UK. And worse. A couple of times, she told me that maybe things would be easier for everyone if she just killed herself. At first when she made that threat, I texted or phoned her. Of course I did.

Finally, I realised that that was exactly why she'd said it. So, the next time, I phoned her roommate, Anna, instead. She told Nicki not to be stupid.

She never came close to killing herself.

Every time I attempted to cut off contact, Nicki would say something that would make me feel too guilty or too scared that she would do something stupid, so I would try to find another way to make it work. By this stage, I had started counselling and decided to mention it at a session. I didn't want to make a big deal of it because I was blind to how much of a big deal it already was. Jan was horrified as I explained what had been unfolding in the previous year and almost as horrified at my reasoning behind not cutting off contact: that I felt I should be loving her as Jesus would. She affirmed what I already knew: that I had to cut off contact. She agreed that, yes, Jesus would love her, but Jesus would in no way be a doormat, which was exactly what I was doing. I was letting Nicki abuse me. I was letting her destroy me, and it had to stop.

So, I sent her one last text, feeling that it would be easier to explain why I was cutting off contact instead of just doing it. I said all I needed to say, and then I stopped. I got multiple replies, multiple texts, e-mails, phone calls that I didn't answer. She tried every angle: telling me what a horrible person I was, apologising that she was a horrible person, manipulating, making me believe that other people had been talking about me so I would want to ask her what they had said. It was incredibly difficult to not reply.

It took a few months of resilience before the messages stopped. They gradually decreased: thirty a day to ten a day, to only a couple a day, to every other day, until eventually, they stopped, or at least became so seldom that it was much easier to handle. In this period, I changed jobs (after being made redundant, a blessing in disguise), so she couldn't reach me by e-mail at work.

And finally, I was free.

By no means did I act perfectly or lovingly through the whole process. I know I hurt her and said things that I'm not proud of. I definitely wish that it didn't have to come down to what it did. But it did teach me an invaluable lesson about boundaries.

For a lot of my life, I have let people take advantage of me, believing that I was going the extra mile and being a good Christian. What I was actually doing was devaluing myself. God created us to love. God commanded us to love. But He also created us as people with a heart and a purpose, and it's okay for us to claim that. In fact, we need to live in that truth. Sometimes that means saying no. And sometimes *no* is the most loving word we can say.

I often wonder what would have happened to Nicki if I hadn't enabled her to manipulate and use me. Would she have confronted her issues sooner, before they caused her to become more hurt? Maybe.

I still find it a bit of a difficult line to draw. That line between the place of going the extra mile even if that person wouldn't go there for you and the place of being a doormat. Every situation is different, but I think these are some helpful questions to ask:

- If I do this, will it ultimately benefit this person?
- Do I know I will get hurt if I do this/let this person do it?
- Is this consistently happening with this person?
- Would Jesus really let somebody treat him like this?
- What are my limitations?
- Does this relationship help me to be the person God created me to be, or does it hinder that?
- Am I trying to save this person in my own strength, or do I trust God to do His part?
- Is this a two-sided relationship, or is it constantly me giving?
- Is this relationship taking more than I am able to give?

It's not easy, but deciding not to be a doormat is not an act of selfishness; it is an act of strength.

A completely necessary one at that.

CHAPTER 30

Engraved

... on being forgotten

My name is engraved on His hands.
Not just written in a temporary, careless manner,
but chiselled in His skin, part of His flesh, part of Him.

Forgotten.
   Omitted.
      Neglected.
         Abandoned.
            Left behind.
               Forsaken.

Being forgotten by someone is not a good feeling: All your friends are going to a party, but the host forgot to send your invitation. Your mum was supposed to pick you up, but half an hour has gone by, and she's not here. You see someone you used to know, you prepare to go and say hi, to catch up with them, but they stare straight through you or give you a blank look with no recognition.

Feeling forgotten by people is not good . . . but feeling forgotten by God is even worse. God, who promises to love you, promises never to leave you or forsake you, promises to always be there.

Feeling forgotten by God can be unbearable.

No matter how well we know that God will not forget us, sometimes it doesn't stop us from feeling that He has. The feeling in those times when you've looked around and seen all your friends getting all the things you deeply desire while you just have to watch and be happy for them. Sitting in another pew of another church at another wedding, smiling while trying not to be cynical about the romanticism and love. Watching opportunities roll past and stop by friends, allowing them to step into careers that fulfil them, that they love, while you put on your physio uniform and go into the clinic again. Going to another farewell party for someone heading off on some adventure, off to see new things and have new experiences, while you carry on with your routine.

I have a friend who is a few years older than I am. She and her husband were an amazing couple I loved spending time with. When I met them, they were in their late twenties and ready to start a family. Over the few years that I was closest with them, I witnessed their struggles and pain as the pregnancy tests kept coming back negative. Around them, friends and family seemingly had no problems, popping out kids all over the show. The whole thing began to wear them down, every little bit of hope met with another pang of disappointment, every other person's joy adding another painful stab.

They felt abandoned. They felt forgotten, and they couldn't understand why.

In any circumstance, however good or bad things are, all of us have felt abandoned, lost, forgotten, or passed over at one point or another. And sometimes the devil uses these times to push our buttons.

We've all got buttons; somewhere in the middle of our brains, we've got buttons. Sometimes they are dormant; they just sit there, not getting pressed, not causing any trouble. But when a button is pressed, something happens.

Pop . . . anger; pop . . . doubt; pop . . . fear; pop . . . sadness; pop . . . forgotten.

Sometimes, it's a quick press; something someone says, a memory, things not quite working out, stirring up those feelings before they quickly subside. But other times, it's as if there is a little demon in our heads standing beside the buttons and poking them with great delight—pop, pop, pop, pop—stopping for a little while until we're lulled into that false sense of security, before pressing the button again and again and again—pop, pop, pop, POP, BOOOOOM!

One such time of button-pressing was about a year ago. It was becoming clear to me that the guy I was friends with and had hoped to develop a relationship with had other ideas. As this was sinking in, I was upset, disappointed, fearful, confused. And in that time, the devil took the chance to push my buttons, to highlight my aloneness by telling me that everyone else had someone.

I lived with three others at that stage: two girls and a guy. One of the girls, the one I spent most time with, went overseas for three weeks. The guy didn't spend a lot of time at the flat, as he was preparing to get married a few months later. "He has someone. You don't." Pop. And the other girl had a new friend. Of the male variety. "So does she. You're alone." Pop. They were just getting to know each other, but he was at our place a lot. Every time I came home and saw his car in the driveway, a finger was jabbed on the button. "Alone." Pop. Every time I got home to an empty house, knowing they were on a date and I was home alone, the button was pressed. "ALONE." Pop. Then one of my best friends back home got engaged and asked me to be her bridesmaid. I was happy for her, I really was, but that button was pushed again. POP.

The final press of the button would have been comical if it hadn't hurt so much. I got a text from a friend asking if he could get something delivered to my work that he would pick up. He worked quite close to me but just a bit further out of town, and the delivery company didn't do rural delivery. I was happy to help.

Then he told me that the item to be delivered was one hundred red roses for his soon-to-be fiancée. Awesome. What a delightful feeling—having one hundred red roses delivered to you—that aren't for you. BOOOOOM!

God had remembered everyone else; God had provided for everyone else. Had He just forgotten about me?

I was sitting in church one Sunday, not long after that particular time, feeling a bit sorry for myself and asking God to talk to me, asking Him for something that would remind me that He was still there, that He still cared. During the worship, one of the older women in church stood up to tell the church something that she thought that God wanted to say to us. She began reading from Isaiah 49.

But Zion said, "The Lord has forsaken me, the Lord has forgotten me."

At this point, I was hopeful, thinking that someone knew how I felt.

"Can a mother forget the baby at her breast and have no compassion on the child she has borne?

Then, my hope dropped a bit. I know a lot of people who have had mothers who haven't cared for them, who have forgotten them.

Though she may forget, I will not forget you!

Then I realised that God knows about those mothers too, but that He is not human. His love is not like a human love. He cannot forget because . . .

See, I have engraved you on the palms of my hands . . ."[1]

Some versions that I've read this verse in have said, "I have written your name on the palms of my hands," but I like this so much better, because engraving is so much more permanent than writing. God loves me enough to go through the pain of chiselling my name onto the palm of His hands.

I've always had the tendency to think that it's nothing special, that there are literally billions of names there. Not from a practical point of view (though God would have to have very large hands), but I've often thought that I am nothing special because God loves everyone. If my name were missing from His hand, He probably wouldn't even notice. Growing up in a church, I heard, so many times, that He died for me because He loved me, but I always thought, "But He died for everyone; He didn't just die for me." And yes, He did die for everyone, but C.S. Lewis helped rationalize this one a little bit better for me. He said,

"He died not for men, but for each man. If each man had been the only man made, He would have done no less."[2]

Yes, He died for everyone. Yes, He loves everyone. But He loves ME enough that even if there were no one else to save, He *still* would have died to save me. Even if there were no other names to engrave, mine would still be there, etched into the palm of His strong, perfect hand.

I may feel forgotten, but God cannot forget me. He has made me part of Him by engraving my name on His hand, in a place that He sees all the time. I am there; He remembers.

No longer forgotten . . . omitted . . . neglected . . . abandoned . . . left behind . . . forsaken.

Now:
    Remembered.
        Included.
            Wanted.
                Kept.
                    Treasured.
                        Engraved.

CHAPTER 31

Genie in a bottle

... on answering prayers

I don't want to worship a god who acts as a genie in a bottle, succumbing to my every whim and fancy. I want to worship a God who sees around corners, who knows what is coming, who knows so much better than I know.

MAC WAS ONE OF MY favourite people in the world.

Mac was funny, often inappropriately, which of course made him funnier. He was kind, valuing and including the people he met, whenever and however he met them. He made great pancakes. He was by no means perfect, and he would be the first to admit it. He was determined, at one stage holding the world record for the longest drumming marathon. He was strong, even right at the end.

I am writing this on the week that would have been Mac's birthday. He always manages to sneak into my thoughts in mid-April, even though it's been nearly four years since he died.

The memories just keep popping up. The time he taught me "Afrikaans," of course using my ignorance to make me say stupid things, such as, "There poops the rabbit." All the times he and his wife Diane welcomed me into their home. The two-day car trip from Port Shepstone to Cape Town with five of us in the car. The time we raced home from town through the gorge after Diane had found a snake in the house. All the times he very convincingly mocked my strong, Northern Irish accent. The many Sunday evenings we would gather at Di and Mac's house for pancakes.

I first met Diane and Michael MacPherson in 2003, on my first trip to South Africa. Diane was in charge of the Scripture Union South Coast, who I would be working for during the six months I was in Port Shepstone. She and Mac would become like family over that time. I stayed with them during my subsequent three trips to South Africa, and they never failed to make room for me, to go the extra mile, and to make me feel completely wanted.

Di and Mac's house felt like home from the instant I walked into it. Mac had built the house himself, and it had so much character. From the wooden key holder saying "The Macs" by the front door, to the fridge that was covered in pictures of the couple, their friends, the places they had travelled to, to the music room that had walls covered in egg boxes, to the lounge that was full of chairs and beanbags to accommodate the many people who came to visit regularly. It was a place where I was completely comfortable and never wanted to leave.

Every Sunday evening, the Macs' house would be overrun with people. Mostly young people from the church, but always a few add-ons as well. Everyone was welcome; no one was excluded. On those evenings, we played volleyball or cards, watched movies, enjoyed each other's company, and ate pancakes. Mac was in charge of pancakes, and it was a pretty big task. At times, there could be about forty people there, and as soon as the pancakes were ready and placed on the table, they would disappear. When it got to the end of the batter, the last pancake would always be a heart-shaped one for Diane. Always.

Those Sunday evenings were some of my favourite times in South Africa, real times of community and fellowship, of fun and laughter, of the important stuff.

Staying with the Macs was one of the things I looked forward to most whenever I spent time in South Africa. They were the kind of people that, after every bit of time I spent with them, I felt more full when I left than when I arrived. They were a special couple.

Mac was diagnosed with lung cancer in 2007 and died a year later after fighting hard. For a long time, I weighed the pros and cons of whether I could and should make the trip back to South Africa to spend some time with him and Di. I can't explain how glad I am that I did, and I'm sure I would regret it to this day if I had made excuses of time and money.

Di and Mac picked me up at the airport before one of Mac's hospital appointments. The first thing he said to me was "You're so white! I'm not even as white as you, and I have cancer!" Ah, the old Mac humour.

I spent a week with them: a week of incredible blessing as I got to share a small part of the journeys of two incredible people. It was a week of things that had become routine for them: specialist appointments, hospital stays, chemotherapy, one night snatched at home before going back to the hospital.

Despite all the circumstances, what I witnessed that week was hope and life. Naturally, there was a lot of sadness, but also real joy. Every day was seen as a blessing by the man who carried on with his life right till the last day. He wasn't the same Mac then as the Mac I'd met four years previously, but he wasn't broken and defeated. He had an amazing serenity and wisdom about him. I remember one night talking to the couple about some boy dramas I had going on. Mac had just taken the morphine that allowed him some mild relief from the pain. In that morphine-induced daze, he gave me better, more sensible, wiser advice about my petty problems than anyone else had.

His attitude was inspiring: often he would be the strong one while everyone around him was fighting to hold it together. All around him, his friends were questioning and declaring how unfair it all was. He was the one with the peace and faith. He had faith that he could be healed, but if not, there was a reason; he would be going to a better place, anyway. I think those are things that Christians feel they should say, when sometimes they feel exactly the opposite, but with Mac, well, I could tell they weren't just words for him. It was obvious that he knew they were true.

I had a lot of questions when Mac got sick. It didn't make any sense to me. Why would God take someone like Mac? Mac, who had so much to offer the world. Mac, who had influenced so many people. Mac, who was talented, funny, kind, generous. Why?

I guess, if anything, I learned that it doesn't always make sense, but even when it doesn't, God is still good and I must still worship Him. Because if we only trust Him and worship Him when times are good and all our prayers are answered, when He does what we think He should, He's no more than a genie in a bottle, controlled by our whims.

I don't want to worship a god like that.

I don't want to worship a god who is controlled by me, because I know how often I mess up, how often I get things wrong. Really, I'd rather leave my life in the hands of someone who knows what He is doing, someone who sees the big picture, even when I don't understand it—someone who sees around the corners.

When Shadrach, Meshach, and Abednego were about to be thrown into the fiery furnace, they said, "If we are thrown into the blazing furnace, the God whom we serve is able to save us . . . but even if He doesn't, Your majesty can be sure that we will never serve your gods or worship the gold statue you have set up." Their attitude was not, "God is able to save us and if He does, we will fall down and worship Him, but if He doesn't, we will find a new god to worship." It was not, "if God doesn't save us, He clearly doesn't love us." It was not, "I'll have faith when I see the results."

It was simply "we trust in God's power, we have faith that He is mighty to save, and we are confident that even if He doesn't answer our prayers in a way we expect, He has a reason and a higher plan; therefore, we will trust and serve and worship."[1]

It's not easy. It's so easy to say those words, to say that you will trust God no matter what, but when faced with something huge, with something that breaks your heart and throws your world into chaos, it's so difficult to stand up and praise God and declare that He is good and just and right and wise and kind. So, in saying this, I'm not denying that it is difficult. Sometimes it's all you can do to get out of bed in the morning, but remember if you can, God sees. He sees your heart. He sees your pain. He sees your struggle. And He sees around the corner. He knows what's coming.

Death is never easy. It was never meant to be easy. Maybe it was never meant to make sense. And I miss Mac, but the end isn't what I remember. What I remember is his journey, his life, his hope.

It was a privilege to be a part of it.

I'm just sorry if you never got to eat his pancakes.

CHAPTER 32

524 photos

... on remembering

In this world, it's too easy to see the darkness. So sometimes, we have to look back to remember how to turn on the light switch.

ONE OF THE THINGS I learned about South Africans during my first seven months there was that they love to give speeches. Birthdays, baptisms, leaving parties, whatever. Someone always has some wise or meaningful words.

Just before I left South Africa the first time, I had a little gathering for some of the people who had been a big part of my life. People I had laughed with, eaten (a lot) with, prayed with, had adventures with, served with. After eating far too much amazing food, there was some time for people to say a few words. At the time, I was super uncomfortable with all the attention on me, but eight years later, I realise how much it meant because I can still clearly see where everyone was sitting and hear the words they said.

Erica, my South African mum, said the words that I remember the most clearly. I was sitting on the floor beneath the TV, beside Shelly. Erica was standing by the armchair, to my right.

And she told me to remember.

She read Philippians 4:8. *Fix your thoughts on what is true and honourable and right and pure and lovely and admirable. Think about things that are excellent and worthy of praise...*[1]

She told me to remember those things, to remember the things that God had done while I was in South Africa, the prayers He had answered, the ways He had changed me and helped me grow. And I have. Those months were a pivotal time in my life, a time that I often refer back to when I'm having a hard time feeling God or trusting that He knows the plan and has my back.

Sometimes, you have to look back.

Now, I'm not saying that we should get stuck in the past, dwelling on it and not letting go of it. But sometimes the world just simply stinks, and life makes us forget. Circumstances can cover the past and make the present look dark and cold and ugly and painful and frustrating and sad and cruel. Things that momentarily appear to be truths make lies of the past, mocking what we've believed.

So sometimes, when you can't see anything but black ahead, you have to look back to see the light.

The things in that verse in Philippians, they seem pretty contrary to the things we see around us every day. How often do you really see truth and honour, purity, loveliness, things that are worthy of admiration, things of excellence, worthy to be praised? Honestly? Probably not often.

But maybe they do happen; maybe it's just far too easy to forget about them. It got me thinking. Thinking of when I've seen those things—things that give me a little bit of hope in humanity and hope in God, in goodness. Let me share some things with you.

True

It can be hard sometimes to believe that the things God says about us, the things He says *to* us, are true. Things like that He has a plan for our lives (Jeremiah 29:11)[2], that we are precious to Him (Isaiah 43:4)[3], and that He delights in us (Zephaniah 3:17).[4]

I saw and believed the truth of these things when I lost my job. Despite my worry, the right job came up in just the right time and at that time, it was so clear to me that God's words were true, that they are always true. He does love me. He does care for me. He does have my life in His hands. And when the world seems to contradict that, I need to look to those times when I have known the truth of His words.

Honourable

It took me a while to think of something to write here. Maybe our society is not a place where honour is easy. I thought long and hard of people I knew and things they had done, and after considering those far and wide, I realised that I needed to come back a little closer to home.

I've always had a lot of love and admiration for my grandparents. Their faith has always been inspirational; they are true people of God. I remember how, when I was growing up, they kept introducing me to people who were around my parents' age and whom they talked about as if they were part of the family. I was so confused about who these people were. My grandparents almost treated them like they treated my mum and her sisters, but they couldn't all be my aunts and uncles: there were so many of them!

As I got older, I started to understand that they had been foster children of my grandparents. Granny and Grandpa had opened their home to more than a hundred children over the years: children who maybe wouldn't have had a lot of other good influences in their lives. They sacrificed a lot to love these kids, to support them and give them a family.

Their love made them people who were full of honour.

Right

My good friend, Olivia, earned a degree in dance. New Zealand is not the easiest country for creative people and performers to find paid work in. It's small, with no huge market for the arts, so after finishing her degree, the opportunities for Olivia were not very great. Shortly after graduating, she was offered a huge opportunity by one of NZ's important choreographers to perform in a high profile dance show.

The problem was that the dancing was going to be burlesque. Think raunchy, small costumes, slightly embarrassing to watch. Maybe it makes the point if I tell you that the choreographer had initially wanted to cast strippers to perform in the show. Olivia had a choice to make. It was something that could boost her career immensely. After a bit of turmoil, she turned it down. It was the right thing to do, even though it was difficult.

Seeing the photos of the performance after it happened, we all knew she had done the right thing!

Pure

David's family has always loved Mercedes cars. His dad has always wanted to own one, but the family has never had enough money. For as long as David can remember, it's been his dream to bless his parents by buying them a nice car. When he moved back to Hamilton after university, he started hunting for a car. He desperately wanted to be able to give his parents a Merc, but any decent ones were WELL out of his price range.

He found one in Auckland, which he went to have a look at. It was a good car, but although he didn't know the price, he knew it was unlikely that he would be able to afford it. As the owner was showing it to him, he asked David why he wanted to buy it. David explained that he wanted it for his parents, describing his family's love of Mercs. David was straight up with the owner and told him that, although it was what he was looking for, he probably didn't have the right money. It didn't take the owner long to tell him that he had recently been baptised, and as a result, he wanted to do a good thing for someone else. After hearing David's reasoning behind wanting the car, the owner asked him how much he had. David told him that he had the money that he'd gotten from selling his old, beat up Honda plus a little bit extra.

The owner said, "That'll do." He just wanted to bless someone with the car, no ulterior motives. David, though shocked, bought the car and drove it to his parents, who were both shocked and delighted.

All because of one man's pure intentions.

Lovely

It doesn't take too much to remind myself of loveliness. I believe I have been in some of the loveliest places in the world. Beautiful places that were created to be beautiful, whose purpose is to show the glory of God merely by showing their beauty. You'll see what I mean if you look up some of these places. In New Zealand, see Cape Reinga, Hahei, Cathedral Cove, Queenstown, Omapere. In Northern Ireland, there's Portstewart, the Giant's Causeway, the Mourne Mountains. In South Africa, check out Oribi Gorge, the Drakensburg Mountains, Table Mountain in Cape Town. In Scotland, you don't want to miss Iona, Rest-and-Be-Thankful. I could go on and on about the loveliness that is all around.

Admirable

When I first arrived in New Zealand, I found it difficult to get to know people. I found that people were very friendly but almost a bit unwilling to go beyond superficial friendliness. They were very willing to talk to me and be friendly for five minutes after church, but I found that very few people invited me to things or appeared to actually want a friendship. Until I met Kirsty. We met one night at church and straight away, she asked if I wanted to grab a coffee the following Sunday before church. It turned into a bit of a regular thing; for a few months, the routine was chai latte at Starbucks and then on to church. Kirsty had plenty of other friends; she didn't need to hang out with me. But she did.

It wasn't until much later that I found out what a difficult time that had been for her. She had been going through some huge things, things that probably would've made me want to curl up in a ball and just avoid people. But instead, Kirsty chose to make life easier for a lonely little foreigner.

And I admire that hugely.

Excellent

When I first met Jared, he was working in a shop at, a job he didn't really love. He also dabbled in photography and videography, and it was very obvious that he had talent. He hadn't had any formal training; he just played around with cameras, improvised when special equipment was required, and spent as much time as he could doing the thing he loved.

On the night of the Rugby World Cup final in 2011, thousands of people gathered in the Fanzone in Auckland to watch the All Blacks beat France. Jared was there, but he wasn't watching the teams play; he was filming the reactions of the crowd. Afterwards, he edited his work into a short clip that he posted online.[5] It went viral. It was crazy. I kept seeing the video pop up on the Facebook pages of friends whom I knew didn't know Jared. People loved the emotion it captured, loved the looks on fans faces as their team won.

Things continued to escalate. The clip has since been used in TV adverts and Sky TV ended up buying the rights to Jared's film for the next eight years.

I love seeing how God took something small—one guy's ideas and passions—and from it, He created something huge.

Something excellent.

Worthy of praise

I have to come back to Mac for this one. And Diane. Because what they went through and the way they responded to it is worthy of praise. Through the difficult diagnosis, the pain, the disappointment, the frustration, the sadness, the fear, the appointments, the scan, the chemo, the radiotherapy, the hospital visits, the loss, Mac was strong and full of life. And Diane was there supporting him, loving him, doing whatever it took.

They didn't get trapped in their own bubble either. Diane had a group of about fifty people that she texted and e-mailed to keep them up-to-date with what was happening. Di and Mac knew that there were people all around the world who cared about Mac, and they didn't shut any of them out. Through the whole process, they went on loving, caring, hoping, carrying on.

That is praiseworthy.

524 photos

I recently ordered copies of many of the photos that I've taken since I arrived in New Zealand. That's 524 photos. My plan is to put them into a scrapbook along with some things I've gathered over the last four years: newspaper clippings, wedding invitations, rugby tickets (I'm a bit of a hoarder). Partly because I like being creative, but more importantly, because I want to remember. I want to look at photos of Kerryann's wedding and remember that some things are worth travelling for 46 hours to get to. I want to look at photos of my first flat in New Zealand and Lee and Sarah, my flatmates, to remind myself how God has been providing for me from the start. I want to look at photos of sunsets and see that God created that beauty, and He created me and thinks that I am just as beautiful. I want to look at New Year's self-take photos where we all look like we haven't slept or washed for three days but are clearly laughing till our stomachs hurt.

Sometimes the world is a hideous place. In those times, it's good to remember the things that make it a little brighter.

CHAPTER 33

The distance between

... on thin places

There are places on Earth that I can't explain.
I don't know why the wind whispers more of God's voice,
the mountains stand in more of His glory, the trees applaud more
of His splendour, the sun proclaims more of His joy. I don't know
why these places show His presence all the more, but I do know
they exist. I have seen them.

MY MUM SPENT MOST OF her life working as a secondary school English teacher, a job that she loved and hated. While she was teaching, she tried out other things: interior design, writing, learning more languages, a lot of travelling, but for as long as I remember, the only thing she wanted to do was to run a bed & breakfast. And I don't think I saw her at peace until that was what she was doing.

For a few years now, she has been running Strumhor B&B in Connel, on the West Coast of Scotland. It's a beautiful place in the area of Scotland where the highlands meet the lowlands. The B&B sits on the shore of Loch Etive, overlooking the Falls of Lora. At the front of the house is a conservatory, which gives views of the falls and beyond to the islands of Lismore and Mull to the West and the immense mountain, Cruachan, to the East. The sunsets across the islands in summer are spectacular, the kind that light up the whole sky and reflect off the seas to engulf everything in sight.

I love going to visit my mum there. It's such a treat just to sit in the conservatory and watch the water flow by, and wait to spy herons and seals and otters. Often when I visit, we'll explore the area, taking small ferries out to the islands or climbing a bit of a mountain (before going for a coffee). One time, we took a five-minute ferry ride over to the small island of Easdale. That day, there was a wedding on the island, so as we strolled around the island (a twenty-minute round trip), we were serenaded by bagpipes. It was a stunning Scottish experience.

My favourite trip was one that I will remember for a long time. We had planned to do it a couple of times previously, but one thing or another stopped us—the ferries were cancelled because of the weather or we had to stay at the B&B to let guests in, but eventually, on my last trip there, the week before I left for New Zealand, everything was perfect for us to make the trip to the island of Iona.

To get there, we took a ferry from Oban to the Isle of Mull, drove about an hour across Mull, and then took another ferry to Iona. The sky had been looking dull and cloudy when we crossed to Mull; there were a few smatterings of rain as we drove, but when we landed on Iona, the clouds divided and we were bathed in sunshine radiating from bright blue skies. The white sand and sun made the sea turn a bright aquamarine, and it was hard to imagine the place ever being anything but bright and clear.

Iona has always been a significant place in Celtic Christianity. It is said to be the place where St Columba landed when he was exiled from Ireland. There, he established a monastery. Now, Iona Abbey, built in 1203, is a significant feature on the island. Mum and I walked through the Abbey, and I remember feeling an incredible serenity. I had left South Africa a few days previously after a difficult and heart-wrenching trip, and a week later I would move my life to the other side of the world. Serenity was not something that came naturally at that point. But being there felt like closing my eyes and taking a refreshingly deep breath.

There was something that I experienced on Iona that I was not alone in discovering. I've since come across many people's accounts of the tranquillity they have felt there. Many have experienced a new level of spiritual peace on the island.

Iona is a thin place.

Sylvia Maddox, a workshop leader in the area of prayer and spirituality, explains "thin places." "There is a Celtic saying that heaven and earth are only three feet apart, but in the thin places, that distance is even smaller. A thin place is where the veil that separates heaven and earth is lifted and one is able to receive a glimpse of the glory of God."[1]

I have experienced a few of these thin places in my life, places where it feels like I can see God and hear His voice all the clearer. In South Africa, my thin place was Jericho's Walls. It was a spot in the gorge that was easy to pass if you didn't know it was there. If you knew of its existence, it was impossible to pass. If you did pull over, the view that would greet you was one that would steal your breath. A sharp edge and shear drop led to a dark green covering of trees that gave way to high rock faces that looked like half-collapsed walls. Beyond them, the carpet of dark green continued, eventually sweeping down to the winding Umzimkulu River before lifting on the other side of the river to mirror the jagged gorge walls.

I think the thing about it was the silence. Sitting on the edge of the gorge, it felt like the surrounding air was weighing heavy on my ears to block out all external noises. It felt like every breath I took in and out was significant, planned. And no matter the turmoil going on outwardly, the weighty air brought a relieving escape and a clarity, because in that place, where I was conscious of every breath of mine, I could feel the whisper of God's breath.

Maybe they seem like places to escape to, places away from everything that comes with the stress of life. I think that's okay. I think it's not just okay, but it's actually good and important to have those escapes. Of course, you have to go back into the normal world of every day eventually, but being in a place that feels so close to heaven makes that everyday life more livable, more manageable, more colourful.

There have been times when it's felt like my brain has a million little people in it, all yelling at each other and fighting for attention. It has felt as if the only way to calm them down is to take them to a place of heavy silence, a place of beauty, a place where waves crash and wind soothes and sunlight heals and the sky calms. In those things, in that creation, it's in them that you see the Creator, that you feel Him, that heaven and earth seem a little bit closer together.

Find a thin place. It could be one of the best things you can do for your soul.

CHAPTER 34

Too much information?

... on vulnerability

To open up is a risk; to lock everything behind closed doors an even greater one.

LAST WEEK, I WAS WATCHING an episode of *The Glee Project*[1], my latest guilty pleasure. A brief summary of how it works if you've never seen it . . . there are initially fourteen contestants, selected from hundreds who auditioned. Out of these fourteen, one will win a role on *Glee*, the hugely popular TV series. Each week, the contestants are given a theme and have to learn vocals and dance routines to a song that characterizes the theme. They shoot a video for the song, and the three contestants with the weakest performances are chosen to sing to stay in the competition. Each week, one is eliminated.

Last week, the theme was vulnerability. The contestants had to perform REM's "Everybody Hurts" and portray a video about bullying. It was interesting to watch what came up as they discussed their experiences with bullying, as victims and, in some cases, as bullies. To be fair, they're all auditioning to be actors, so I didn't get so sucked in that I believed every word out of their mouths, but what was more interesting to me was the varying degrees of willingness to be vulnerable. Some of them relished the opportunity to share and opened up freely. Others took a little more nudging. Others needed several hard shoves before giving any details that might expose who they really were.

It made me think about which one of them I would be. If I was asked about my experiences with bullying or heartbreak or fear or disappointment or family, would I tell freely? Or would I take a bit more coaxing? Or would I keep some things so closely guarded that everyone would think my life had been pretty sweet? Maybe, having read this book, it seems to you like a silly thing for me to say. I've shared a lot throughout these chapters, but in some ways, this is easy. Though I want people to read it, though I'm writing in hope it will be read, right now, it's me and my computer. It's easy to open up to a computer. Much easier than opening up to a person sitting in front of me and looking into my eyes.

I tried to make a list of people I believe that I was totally honest and vulnerable with. After a fair bit of thought, the list only had one person on it. Yes, there were other people who I have been vulnerable with at times, but on the whole, I have my shiny, happy face on and my walls up around them. So, what is it that's different about David?

David is a colleague from work. Well, that's how he started. Now, he's a good friend, someone I feel refreshed around. But, how does he permit me to be vulnerable? Well, first of all, he is incredibly accepting. He has known rejection, and I think, in that, you can go one of two ways. One is to reject everyone around you out of bitterness, and the other is to make an even bigger effort to accept everyone. He is also very encouraging. He encourages my thoughts. When I write stuff, he tells me when it's good. He tells me I have a gift. All that makes me want to open up.

I always thought of myself as an open and vulnerable person, but in making that list, I see that it's not the case, at least not to the extent that I thought it was. I've tried to think back, to see if there was a time when I had a different degree of vulnerability and if so, what changed. I've come to some conclusions.

I went through a cycle of vulnerability as I was growing up. In my early teens, I was closed; toward my late teens, I swung to the opposite extreme; as I approached my twenties, I gradually edged back the other way, settling somewhere on the closed side of just right.

My parents divorced when I was seven, and through my last few years of primary school, it was a source of embarrassment more than anything for me. Back then, divorce wasn't nearly as common as it is now, and I didn't know enough people with divorced parents to even know what divorce was. As a result, I kept quiet about it, suppressing the facts and therefore the feelings.

When I started high school, I began to realise that, instead of embarrassment, I could actually use my family situation as a source of sympathy. "Poor little Philippa with the divorced parents. Life must be hard for her." I liked the attention, so gradually, I began to open up more and more, telling people the intimacies of how hard life was and how that made me feel. I would almost tell anyone who listened for long enough. I wasn't afraid to cry in front of strangers or people I knew, as long as they comforted me.

When Tim and Laura started dating, and that hurt overwhelmed me, I began to sink deeper into that self-pity and into trying to get others to pity me too. For me, one used to being second best, used to sinking into the background, pity was better than nothing, better than being ignored. But, by this stage, I had friends who cared but who would not tolerate my moping. If I sat in the corner with my sad face, they would often ignore me and occasionally tell me to get over it. And I don't blame them. A sympathy-seeker is not a fun person to be around. But it took me a long time to work that out. In the process, I would simply push harder and harder, becoming sadder and more pathetic, almost to the point of alienating myself from others.

Eventually, what happened was that I told myself that my friends didn't care that I was sad. Actually, they did; they just didn't care when I put on my fake sad face (whether or not I knew it was fake) to get attention. They would get annoyed with me. I thought I was just plain annoying. They would ignore my real and fake feelings, so I would ignore my feelings. They would tell me to build a bridge, so I built a bridge high above the raging rapids, which didn't make the rapids go away. I repressed all my feelings, trying not to show any of them. I think I just wasn't sure where the line was, wasn't sure when it was okay to tell people I was sad and when it would just come across as needy and annoying.

Maybe I haven't even fully worked it out yet. One thing I've noticed that I do now is constantly say I'm fine. Even when I do open up to people, I'll always finish it off with a positive statement. "One of my friends is getting married back at home today, and it kills me that I'm not there, but it's all good." "My heart has been broken, I feel like I'm going to be alone forever and I'm really lonely, but I'm sure it'll all be fine."

I'm still learning.

That's just part of my process of learning the right level of vulnerability, and there are a million other things that can affect it. Some people feel they have to hold everything together because if they fall apart or show weakness, someone close to them will lose faith in them, or someone close to them will fall apart themselves. Then there are those who have always been seen as the strong one and don't want anyone to think differently. And there are those who haven't even let themselves think they are vulnerable, convinced there is never anything wrong, and they can't quite work out why they react to things with such anger, why some things make them so sad, why one particular comment sticks with them deep in their souls. Also, there are people who are desperate to be liked, and they think that, to have that, they have to be shiny and happy all the time.

Being vulnerable is a risk. In a fight or a war, the vulnerable area is the one with the least protection, the one that will hurt the most if attacked. To expose that area, you have to trust that the person you're exposing it to is not going to attack it, not going to use it to hurt you. We're human; we make mistakes that hurt each other. When Tim hurt me like he did, it took a lot longer to recover because I had exposed the most vulnerable part of my heart to him, and he struck me deep in that spot.

There is also the risk of being misunderstood. When you open up your heart to people, when you tell them about your dreams and your passions, there is always the risk that they will not understand, which can, in some ways, refute your feelings, maybe even invalidate them. If you keep opening up to people who don't want to understand your heart, eventually you find that it's just less painful to keep it to yourself.

If it's a risk, why should you even bother? And what is the right level of vulnerability? Despite being hurt by it, despite struggling with it, I do think it's important. Sometimes it leads to hurt, but sometimes, I'd like to say more times, it leads to healing. Repressing it all does not make it go away; sharing it is the start of the journey. And if we can manage it, sharing our hearts gives other people permission to do the same.

Having said that, I would also say, do it with wisdom. Don't tell everyone your deepest, darkest secrets, because some people will use them against you. As much as I wish it wasn't true, it is how the world works sometimes. So, just make sure you can trust those to whom you reveal your vulnerability. You may be wrong, but unfortunately, sometimes that is just the risk you need to take.

God has made you who you are. He has used each experience in your life to shape you and build you. Don't hide that person; don't let anyone tell you that person is not enough or is too much. Choose who you open that person up to, but when you've chosen, do it.

In vulnerability, there is healing, there is hope, there is life.

CHAPTER 35

It goes on

... on life

Stand there in the crowd and bawl your eyes out if you need to. But when you're done, dry your tears, join that line once more, and keep on going.

STANDING IN O.R. TAMBO INTERNATIONAL Airport in Johannesburg, a city where I knew no one, in a line with about 300 other people whose flight had just been cancelled, I thought it couldn't get any worse.

I was trying to fly back to Heathrow, from where I would fly on to Belfast and spend a night at home before flying to Scotland to visit my mum for a week before I was due to leave home to go to New Zealand.

That was the plan.

Earlier that day, I had said goodbye to my friends in Port Shepstone, feeling like I was leaving a little bit of my heart behind, not being sure when I might be back to pick it up again. I had flown from Durban to Johannesburg that morning, leaving myself more than enough time to catch my evening flight to Heathrow. When I went to check in, the friendly looking member of staff informed me that the poor old pilot was sick and was unable to fly the plane. "Surely they would have a backup!" I hear you cry. Well, they did, sort of. There were, in fact, a couple of backups, however, one had already reached his flying quota for the day, and the other could not be located.

The friendly member of staff advised me to proceed to the airline help desk, where I would be informed of the options and procedures. I followed his advice. Having been at the airport well before the flight was due to depart, there weren't too many people in the line at that stage. Somehow, it still managed to take about an hour to get to the head of the line to talk to someone. A stressed looking member of staff advised me that they didn't quite know what was happening yet, gave me a temporary ticket, and told me to come back to the desk around 8pm.

At 7:30pm, there were about 300 people in that line waiting to get to that desk. Gradually, the mutter went down the line that the flight had definitely been cancelled. This was one of my worst nightmares. Flying stressed me. Flying alone stressed me more. Being stranded in an airport in a city where I knew no one stressed me most.

Eventually, after, I don't know how long, I got to the head of the line again, to the same stressed member of staff. She told me the flight was cancelled. I told her that I knew that. She told me that I would have to wait. I told her that she had given me a temporary ticket earlier and asked if that meant anything. She sighed and glanced at the ticket. After looking at her computer and adding a few details, she told me to go to the check-in desk of another airline that was also flying to Heathrow that night. She guaranteed nothing, but told me that there was a possibility of getting on that flight. Some of the stress started to fade.

I ran over to the check-in desk of said other airline and handed them the ticket, smiling with every ounce of hope I had. The grumpy-looking member of staff informed me that the ticket did not state what class I was supposed to be travelling and that I would have to go back to the help desk again. I stared at him open-mouthed for a few seconds, half believing that he would break into a smile and say, "Haha, just kidding!" He didn't. So, I started to walk away, not quite sure what was next. There had been a man standing behind me who was in the same situation as I was. When he heard what the grumpy-faced member of staff had said, he whispered to me, "Just write this letter in this box; that's what they've done on mine," pointing to the box that stated that he was travelling in economy class. I snuck off to the side and wrote the letter in the box before bounding back up to the grumpy member of staff. The helpful man had just gone through the gate to get on the flight. The grumpy member of staff looked at me and said, "I'm sorry; this flight is now full."

It took me a good few minutes to register what he said and what had just happened. My last option for getting to Heathrow that night was gone. I had no idea what the next option was. Was I meant to sleep in airport? Would they throw us all out onto the street? Would they manage to find space for 300 of us on other flights? Why was this happening?!

For the third time, I went to stand in the line to get to the help desk.

And at that moment, I did what any reasonable person would do in that situation: I burst into tears. I stood there, holding my thirty kilograms of luggage, and I just started to cry uncontrollably. You know how some people, when they cry, they look forlorn and hauntingly beautiful? I am not one of those people. My face was red, my eyes were screwed up, my nose was streaming. And I didn't care.

I was pretty sure that things couldn't get any worse. Blow after blow after disappointment after knock after frustration: I was stuck.

So, what happened next?

I'll tell you . . . life went on.

The airline arranged shuttles to a local hotel. On the shuttle, I met someone else who was flying the exact same route as I was to Belfast. A group of us were taken to dinner (courtesy of the airline), before spending a night in a hotel that had a large spa bath and huge, comfortable bed in each room. The following morning, a shuttle was provided back to the airport, where we were all put on a flight to Heathrow with a perfectly healthy pilot. When I got to Heathrow, it was too late for a flight to Belfast that night, so the airline provided another hotel with more free food and more free transfers, and eventually, 24 hours after I was meant to, I landed at Belfast City Airport with a sigh of relief.

Life went on and it worked out.

There have been many times, so many times, times that I've spoken about in these last chapters when all I've wanted to do is stop in the midst of the crowd and cry. When I've felt like there's no one to help, like nothing is working out, like it's all just too difficult.

But you know what? In every one of those times, every single one, life has gone on and it has worked out. Maybe I haven't always seen the ways it has worked out until much later, but here I am, still standing.

Nobody ever promised that life would be easy, that it would be a straight road, that there wouldn't be ups and downs, twists and turns, speed bumps and roundabouts. And I am not going to promise you that either. But I want to ask you to please, please, not give up. Stand there in that crowd and bawl your eyes out if you need to. That's okay! But when you're done, dry your tears, join that line once more and keep on going.

You'll get home eventually.

Epilogue

further along the road

AND NOW...

Reading through the final edit of this book, there was so much I thought about changing. These words have come gradually over the last few years. A lot of the things I felt and wrote about are things I don't feel any more. Should I have left them out?

I think that if I had, a lot of the point of the book would be lost. The fact that I can see the change: change in my thoughts, my feelings, my life; that is what makes the journey bearable, what keeps me going.

And what I want most of all is for that to keep other people going as well. For so much of my life, as I've gone through these things, I've believed that I was the only one, that nobody else had these problems and that therefore, I was the problem. Even as I've written and especially as I've gone through and edited, I've heard these voices asking me what on earth I was thinking, telling me that I can't let other people see this side of me because it is my issue, my problem, no one else has them.

Writing this book has been a painful process. Some of these chapters would never have been written without the pain that inspired them. They have been born from pain, but in some ways, the writing has soothed and defeated and healed that pain. The writing has given the pain a purpose, helped it make sense. I deeply hope that every hurt that I've gone through might help to ease the hurts of someone else, help them know that they're not the only one and that there will be an end, that *"even the darkest night will end and the sun will rise."*[1]

My sun is rising, the sun whose existence I had started to doubt, I can see it now.

I always hoped for healing, but I always hoped with a great amount of skepticism. But now, the things I hoped for, they're coming to be. The place I am at now, I feared and doubted that I would ever get here.

I still have a long way to go. I am, by no means, completely and perfectly whole. I know I never will be, till He comes, but I'm heading in the right direction.

Over the speed bumps and around the roundabouts.

Notes

PROLOGUE

Chapter 1. I am the sum of my story
1. My mum used to call me Philly Milly. Thanks, mum.
2. This is a phrase often used to refer to the time in Northern Ireland when the fighting between Protestant groups and Catholic groups was at its worst. It would take many pages to accurately explain all the history behind this, but the period of The Troubles was a time of segregation, fighting, bombs, fear, shooting, and disharmony in the extreme.
3. http://suni.co.uk; www.su.org.za ; www.scriptureunion.org.uk All accessed on 20/07/13.

Chapter 2. Stepping over the edge
1. Now the George Best Belfast City Airport.
2. About ten others who were also going to be spending time in various areas of South Africa with SU.
3. www.oribigorge.co.za/wild5.html Date accessed: 20/07/13.

Chapter 3. Under Construction
1. Published by Scripture Union UK, available for download from http://www.scriptureunion.org.uk/162923.id#.UeiXOBxoEzA Date accessed: 19/07/13.

231

2. 2 Corinthians 12:9, NIV.
3. Philippians 1:6, NLT.
4. From *A Woman of No Importance* by Oscar Wilde, 1893.

Chapter 4. Things I learned from movies and why they're not true
1. The author of this quote is unknown.
2. Walt Disney Productions, 1950.
3. Walt Disney Productions, 1937.
4. Walt Disney Productions, 1959. Incidentally, I think *Sleeping Beauty* scarred me for life. How scary is it when Maleficent turns into that big dragon thing??
5. Walt Disney Pictures, Silver Screen Partners IV, 1989.
6. Walt Disney Feature Animation, Walt Disney Pictures, 1996.
7. *He's Just Not That Into You*, New Line Cinema, 2009.

Chapter 5. Shalom and Sehnsucht
1. *Strong's Exhaustive Concordance of The Bible,* # 7965, by Dr James Strong, 1890.
2. Mr Lewis said in his autobiography, *"Surprised by Joy",* 1955 that "The strange English accents with which I was surrounded seemed like the voices of demons."
3. *The Weight of Glory and Other Addresses,* C.S. Lewis. First Published by Eerdmans, 1965.
4. *Pilgrim's Regress,* C.S. Lewis. First published by J.M. Dent and Sons, 1933.
5. *The Last Battle,* C.S. Lewis. First published by The Bodley Head, 1956.

Chapter 6. Every new beginning comes from some other beginning's end
1. "Closing Time," Semisonic, released 1998 from the album, *Feeling Strangely Fine,* record label MCA, written by Dan Wilson.

2. From *Grey's Anatomy*, "A change is gonna come," 2007, written by Shonda Rhimes.

Chapter 7. Sometimes you know . . . sometimes you don't

1. The main funding body for accidents and injuries in New Zealand had reduced funding for physio, meaning that patients had to pay for physio treatment, which had previously been free of charge. This, of course, meant that private physio practices initially lost a lot of clients.
2. I worked as an event security guard, a receptionist, a shop assistant, a rugby and football physio and wrote a few articles for a magazine.
3. The full quote reads, *"Love God and do whatever you please: for the soul trained in love to God will do nothing to offend the One who is Beloved."* St Augustine of Hippo, http://www.goodreads.com/quotes/622083-love-god-and-do-whatever-you-please-for-the-soul Accessed on: 19/07/13.

Chapter 8. In search of the greenest grass

1. Read the entire book of Jonah in the Bible. It's a short book.

Chapter 9. Swings, slides and seesaws

1. Travel, stay single, move away, have pizza . . . just kidding!
2. Jeremiah 29:11, NIV.

Chapter 10. Fuzzy feelings and arranged marriage

1. 1 Corinthians 13, NIV.
2. "Do You Love Me?" from *Fiddler on the Roof*, 1971, MGM, Produced by The Mirisch Corporation, Cartier Productions. Source: http://www.imdb.com/title/tt0067093/?ref_=fn_al_tt_1 Accessed on: 19/07/13.

Chapter 11. "Pongs" about mixed signals

1. http://dictionary.reference.com/browse/flirt?s=t . Accessed on: 19/07/13.
2. If you want to make this a song, please feel free.

Sometimes they even sing a little "Pippalicious" song.

Chapter 12. Kelly and Hannah
1. www.myersbriggs.org Accessed on: 19/07/13.
2. http://animalinyou.com Accessed on: 19/07/13.
3. www.half-asleep.com/pooh/interact/quiz/quiz.php Accessed on: 19/07/13.
4. www.brainfall.com/quizzes/which-disney-princess-are-you/ Accessed on: 19/07/13.
5. www.youthink.com/quiz.cfm?obj_id=109980 Accessed on: 19/07/13.
6. This theory dates back to Ancient Egypt and Mesopotamia, before Hippocrates incorporated it into medicine.

Chapter 13. From Lynne to David
1. She always beat me.
2. Rachel and I lost touch after school, and I have no idea where she is. I would love to apologise to Rachel for treating her like I did. Maybe this is a start.
3. If you're interested (I know you are), Ruthie was the thumb, Cat the middle finger, Julie the ring finger and Kerryann the little finger.
4. However, we are not crazy cat ladies. Well, maybe a little.

Chapter 14. My cup overflows
1. Pastor Steven Furtick, Elevation Church, Charlotte, NC. Source: https://twitter.com/stevenfurtick/status/67981913746444288 Accessed on 19/07/13.
2. The exam that UK students do at the end of fifth form, at the age of 16.

Chapter 15. No feeling . . . no hurt
1. www.thefreedictionary.com/apathy. Accessed on: 19/07/13.
2. "Need You Now," Lady Antebellum. Released 24th August 2009, Capitol Nashville. Written by Lady Antebellum and Josh Kear.

Chapter 16. Depression
1. *Emotionally Free* by Grant Mullen M.D. Chosen, September 2003.

Chapter 17. The fingers of a 500-pound gorilla
1. The Gate Control Theory of Pain, Melzack, R. and Wall, P., 1965, *Science,* "Pain Mechanisms: A New Theory."

Chapter 18. Getting over it
1. I don't recommend this after a break up!

Chapter 19. A new definition
1. www.summermadness.co.uk Accessed on: 20/07/13.

Chapter 20. An Olympic silver medal
1. www.strumhor.co.uk Accessed on: 20/07/13
2. Martin Luther King Jr. 1929-1968 http://www.goodreads.com/quotes/21045-if-a-man-is-called-to-be-a-street-sweeper Accessed on 19/07/13
3. Boris Becker was top seed and two-time defending champion. Peter Doohan was ranked 70th.

Chapter 21. Movie in my mind
1. "I'm not that girl," from *Wicked: The Musical.* Music and lyrics by Stephen Schwartz.
2. Proverbs 4:23, NIV.

Chapter 22. How not to be single
1. Yum

Chapter 23. The control of a situation
1. This process, leading up to and resulting in the Good Friday Agreement of 1998 was, in theory, the end of most of the violence that plagued Northern Ireland for years.
2. Philippians 4:7, AKJV.
3. Philippians 4:7, MSG.

4. Thomas Edison, American inventor and businessman, 1847-1931 http://quotationsbook.com/quote/32668/#sthash.Uyig94Ar.dpbs Accessed on: 19/07/13.

Chapter 24. Those who pluck the fruits at the wrong time
1. The Magician's Nephew, C.S. Lewis, first published by The Bodley Head 1955.

Chapter 25. First of July
1. "Closing Time," Semisonic, released 1998 from the album, Feeling Strangely Fine, record label MCA, written by Dan Wilson.
2. Isaiah 66:9, NCV.
3. "First of July," Foy Vance, from the album Hope, 2008, Wurdamouth Records.

Chapter 26. A God who dangles carrots?
1. The Shawshank Redemption, 1994, Castle Rock Entertainment.
2. 1 Corinthians 13:13, NIV.
3. Aristotle, Greek philosopher 384-322 BC. http://www.goodreads.com/quotes/3987-hope-is-a-waking-dream Accessed on 19/07/13.
4. John Armstrong, Art of Preserving Health (1744), Book IV, line 310 Scottish physician and poet 1704-1774 Source: http://en.wikiquote.org/wiki/Hope Accessed on 19/07/13.
5. Evgeny Baratynsky, Two Fates (1823), translated by Dimitri Obolensky. Russian poet 1800-1844 Source: http://en.wikiquote.org/wiki/Hope Accessed on 19/07/13.
6. Proverbs 13:12, NIV.
7. "Two Shades of Hope," Foy Vance, from the album Hope, 2008, Wurdamouth Records.
8. Samuel Johnson (The Idler, No. 58 (26 May 1759)) Source: http://en.wikiquote.org/wiki/Hope Accessed on 19/07/13.
9. Vaclav Havel (Disturbing the Peace (1986), Chapter 5: The Politics of Hope).

Source: http://en.wikiquote.org/wiki/Hope Accessed on 19/07/13.
10. Zephaniah 3:17 (paraphrased from NIV).
11. Numbers 23:19, NLT.

Chapter 27. Eagles in Zimbabwe
1. From *Grey's Anatomy*, "Scars and souvenirs," 2007, written by Debora Cahn.
2. Isaiah 40:31, TNIV.

Chapter 28. If only you could see yourself as I see you
1. Zephaniah 3:17, TNIV.
2. Isaiah 62:4, TNIV.
3. I John 3:1, NIV.
4. Luke 12:6-7, CEV.
5. Ephesians 2:10, NLT.
6. Psalm 139:14, NIV.

Chapter 29. Confessions of a doormat

Chapter 30. Engraved
1. Isaiah 49: 14-16, TNIV.
2. C.S. Lewis, *Perelandra*, 1943, first published by The Bodley Head.

Chapter 31. Genie in a bottle
1. Daniel, chapters 1-3.

Chapter 32. 524 photos
1. Philippians 4:8, NLT.
2. *For I know the plans I have for you," says the Lord. "They are plans for good and not for disaster, to give you a future and a hope.* Jeremiah 29:11, NLT.
3. *Since you are precious and honored in my sight, and because I love you, I will give people in exchange for you, nations in exchange for your life.* Isaiah 43:4, NIV.

4. *For the Lord your God is living among you. He is a mighty saviour. He will take delight in you with gladness. With his love, he will calm all your fears. He will rejoice over you with joyful songs.* Zephaniah 3:17, NLT.
5. Watch Jared's original video with this link – vimeo.com/31010288

Chapter 33. The distance between
1. Sylvia Maddox, The Mystery of God: Where can I touch the edge of Heaven? 2004 Source: http://www.explorefaith.org/mystery/mysteryThinPlaces.html Accessed on: 19/07/13.

Chapter 34. Too much information
1. *The Glee Project,* created by Ryan Murphy, first aired on Oxygen 2011.

Chapter 35. It goes on

EPILOGUE
1. This is a line from the finale of one of my favourite musicals, *Les Miserables,* by Boublil and Schoenberg.

For more information about
Pip McCracken
&
SPEED BUMPS AND ROUNDABOUTS
please visit:

Website: www.pipmccracken.com
E-mail: pipmwriter@gmail.com
Twitter: @pipmccracken
Facebook: www.facebook.com/PipMccrackenWriter

For more information about
AMBASSADOR INTERNATIONAL
please visit:

www.ambassador-international.com
@AmbassadorIntl
www.facebook.com/AmbassadorIntl